THIS PROJECT IS SUPPORTED BY A GRANT FROM THE NATIONAL ENDOWMENT FOR THE ARTS IN WASHINGTON, D.C., A FEDERAL AGENCY.

INTERNATIONAL STANDARD BOOK NUMBER: 0-935314-25-3
LIBRARY OF CONGRESS CATALOG CARD NUMBER: 83-072931
© 1983 BY THE ART GALLERY, CALIFORNIA STATE UNIVERSITY, FULLERTON
ALL RIGHTS RESERVED

THE HOUSE
THAT ART BUILT

THE MAIN ART GALLERY, VISUAL ARTS CENTER
CALIFORNIA STATE UNIVERSITY, FULLERTON

OCTOBER 28–DECEMBER 7, 1983

WITH ESSAYS BY:
DEXTRA FRANKEL
JAN BUTTERFIELD
MICHAEL H. SMITH

CONTENTS

DIRECTOR'S FOREWORD

It is only through the efforts and cooperation of artists, galleries, museums and collectors that an exhibition of this scope is possible. For so generously lending from their collections, our sincere appreciation goes to Betty Asher, Richard and Rosemary Bergen, Gail and Barry Berkus, Ruth and Tod Braunstein, The Edward R. Broida Trust, Leo Castelli, Frank and Berta Gehry, Edwin Janss and Roselyne and Richard Swig. The following galleries assisted in obtaining information pertinent to individual artists and made requested works available for this presentation: from New York—Leo Castelli, Paula Cooper, Richard L. Feigen & Co., Janis, Max Protetch, Holly Solomon and John Weber; from Los Angeles—Asher/Faure, Flow Ace, Janus, L.A. Louver, Koplin and Neil G. Ovsey; from Dallas—Delahunty; from Chicago—Betsy Rosenfield Gallery, Inc.; and from Washington, D.C.—Middendorf. We are most grateful to these galleries and their representatives for their involvement with the project.

I take this opportunity to especially thank Walter Hopps, Director, The Menil Collection, Houston, for invaluable assistance; Naomi Vine, Museum of Contemporary Art, Chicago, for obtaining the video-taped film by Rudolph Burckhardt (New York) of Charles Simonds' performances; Charmaine Locke for offering the exhibition she organized in 1981, "The Image of the House in Contemporary Art," as a springboard to this exhibit; Michael H. Smith, Pasadena, for his essay contribution in the catalogue; and Jan Butterfield, San Francisco, for the catalogue's major essay. She has captured the richness and depth of expression which is at the core of these artists' works.

However, it is to the artists that I heartily offer my thanks for their belief and participation in this project. Their unanimous support and insightful statements have added spirited energy.

The November 11 symposium, moderated by Jan Butterfield with artist panelists Siah Armajani, Tony Berlant and Roland Reiss, architect Elyse Grinstein and curator Paul Schimmel, promises to be a richly woven tapestry of substantive discernments. Their interaction has further broadened and enriched our exhibition, and, through it, it is our hope that viewers will experience a growing sense of the fiber of art.

In the past decade the prevalent use of the house or architectural setting as an image in art seems to reflect an awareness that a sense of place relates to more than just a setting. It encompasses psychological impact, social nuance and cultural dialogue. Working within an area of historical and contemporary aesthetics, many of today's artists embody a presence understood by viewers through images of shared reality. Their images evoke memories of sound, smell, touch and space, and so become a fragment of reality or a drama that is translated to the viewer's understanding of implied dwelling and architecture. These artists work within an arena of past and present cultures, making references to contemporary architecture by incorporating imagery that is narrative, sociological, psychological or illusionistic.

In the foreword to the catalogue of the 1981 exhibition, "The Image of the House in Contemporary Art," artist and guest curator Charmaine Locke aptly notes:

> The prevalence of this image in recent art is an indication and visual representation of transitions occurring throughout our society. We are seeing a return to humanistic issues, a reevaluation of the personal, the experiential, as sources for art, architecture and other activities within our culture, and a reemerging concern for the impact current acts have on our future destiny.[1]

She further suggests that "artists are portrayers of their times." They have "ability to sense the pulse of the on-going stream, yet at the same time to be precursor, to offer visionary solutions...."[2]

In 1965 the noted architecture historian David Gebhard wrote an article in *Artforum* entitled, "Charles Moore: Architecture and the New Vernacular," in which he states:

> Almost as an answer to the Kahnian lack of concern for *real* structure is the development of a third mode which is intensely involved with architecture as building. The source of inspiration for this mode is the folk vernacular of the 20th century, the non-architect designed structure. The architectural language used is that of ... everyday materials and the conventional way in which these materials are put together.... One of the most forceful exponents of this new vernacularism is the ... architect, Charles Moore.... The apparent casualness of his buildings is entirely due to the source of his architectural language. But once one seriously experiences these buildings it is obvious that he has simply exploited the vernacular language of the non-architect designed building in order to make a highly refined and sophisticated statement.... If one wished to play with analogies, it could be argued that Moore's borrowing of the builder's mode is akin to the use of the found object in contemporary sculpture. In both instances the everyday object—which exists on one level—is employed as a language to make a statement on another level.[3]

1

BY DEXTRA FRANKEL

In order to explore these issues further, "The House That Art Built"[4] has been organized for the art gallery at California State University, Fullerton. This exhibition was developed as part of several presented simultaneously in institutions collaborating with the Craft and Folk Art Museum on the theme of American vernacular architecture. "The House That Art Built" presents works by forty-one contemporary artists who have integrated the essence of environment within their imagery, and whose perception of a common language, translated through a visual dialogue, reflects the idiom of vernacular architecture. Site-specific installations and those environments essential to the concept and intent of this exhibition are documented by means of a multi-image slide and sound presentation.

At the core of this exhibition is the work of H.C. Westermann. While his craftsmanship emanated from early work as a carpenter, his pieces embody intense emotion and vision concerning the human condition. He re-addressed reality through autobiographical reference, drama, humor and intuitive psychological associations in narrative works that incorporate commonplace materials and imagery. Prior to his death in 1981, Westermann wrote the following statement for "The Image of the House in Contemporary Art" exhibition:

> As you will notice, I've designated a house I made for the last 25 years (off and on). I started using this form when it was completely foreign to people in the arts (except for a very few) and sure as hell wasn't very popular. In fact, most people thought I was nuts.
>
> You must understand my inability to explain or even talk about the houses I have made. Perhaps they are based on a lot of things, such as the relationship between the "houses and humanness."[5]

During an interview with sculptor Tony Berlant, it became evident that his involvement with the house image and its underlying implications is also intense.[6] In 1963 he found a birdhouse at the county dump, reinforced it and covered it with tin. From that beginning, more forms developed, less modest in scale. In 1966 he built a "temple" around one of those pieces, leading into much larger architectural works. As their scale increased, his fantasy became one of constructing a building around the temples; between 1966 and 1968 they became buildings within buildings. To him the house is a "totally loaded symbol."[7]

> What could be more powerful? For me it alludes not just to architecture but, more importantly, to the head. The houses always relate to the specificity of each human life, and there's the sense that the form remains the same even though the content varies. It stands for the human presence, while the rectangle in painting alludes to the convention of the window, so the house is a stage—just another kind of convention in which the perimeters of the drama are framed.[8]

Berlant deals with content from the aspect of the houses being homes that convey specific human situations, and he considers them personal fetish-like icons, "like souvenirs of my own life."

When listening to Roland Reiss discuss his work, it is immediately apparent that his approach, too, comes from within years of cumulative thought.[9] The inner drama and life scenario is his concern, and the sets which are created, as in the *Dancing Lessons* series, are variations on a theme to envelop different aspects of a single issue. The subtle nuances between each work within the series are achieved by the seemingly random juxtaposition of similar everyday elements. Proximity, color, scale and visual cues lead the viewer along narrative paths which represent make-believe circumstances or events. It is this creation of fiction from visual imagery that enables Reiss to form content in his work.

> [This creation of] fiction . . . was the beginning of the whole approach for me of content. When you have a fictional situation, then you really make magic. The miniatures in particular work in such a way that they become observed like games that you participate with. . . . As I would reduce things in scale . . . I would get smaller so I could get bigger. It has something to do with the paradigm, with modeling reality. These are all ways of abstracting certain aspects of reality and working things out. That is, you begin to have some control over what is going on in the world and in your own world in particular. Part of the conceptual part of it was that you would have a kind of overview, a placement of things low so you could see the plan, see what's happening from the top as well as the sides.[10]

Inherent in the success of this work is the artist's ability to stimulate and extract personal experience from the viewer. This achievement of a sense of place or movement through time is enhanced not only by attention to minute detail but by Reiss' interest in semiology (the study of signs and codes and how information is communicated). In further discussing the development of content, Reiss notes:

> I was moving from homilies, [then] from clues to cues, [so] that these objects could be different chains of thought, different areas of thinking . . . not quite scenarios yet, but territories of thought that were overlaid and interlocked. . . . The humor that I allow is part, in a way, of bringing these ideas to the surface. . . . While my work carries a heavier content load, I expect it to do its job through the form and talk to you psychologically, through the eye rather than the words . . . because words *never* explain works of visual art. . . . Words [are] only a king of surrounding—[a] support for what's going on here. . . . The term "dancing lessons" really has to do with the dance of life, a very simple metaphor, that we dance under all kinds of circumstances, and when we go to the bank we do the bank dance; we go to the post office and do the post office dance. . . . These [are] rituals, some of them formalizing rituals, some of them rituals in relation to

work . . . that we all perform, choose to perform, and/or [are] compelled to perform. . . . Basically, art is a very beautiful kind of fiction; it's magic made out of practically nothing, and it lives as long as the dance lives.[11]

The attainment of an architectural presence or content is within easy grasp in the works of Westermann, Berlant and Reiss. The forms used, though juxtaposed with abstracts of psychological images, are either literal or archetypal. It is interesting that within the work of Jackie Ferrara, however, the imagery, although more obtuse and less overt, evokes an architectural resonance. There are no windows, columns or absolute box-like forms, yet the interaction occurs. Perhaps one responds to the ordering or mathematical assemblage of the material, the scale or the interaction of its geometric volumes. Recently the laminated wood structures have become enlarged, enabling the negative spaces and smaller courts to form environments to be walked through and experienced.

The definition of vernacular in *Webster's New Collegiate Dictionary* is, ". . . of or relating to, or characteristic of a period, place, or group, esp: of or relating to or being the common building style of a period or place."[12] Siah Armajani uses objects that seem commonplace, powerless and casual in order to orchestrate our involvement with environment.

In a 1981 catalogue essay, Julie Brown notes:

Armajani draws from the forms of architecture and furniture to express philosophical ideas through his art.

Public use gives the work its meaning; sculpture as location, as a place to be, as something to use. These are common values shared by architecture, sculpture and furniture. Their forms shape our surroundings and influence our activities. These disciplines need not be isolated from one another. . . .

. . . The forms, materials and methods of construction are taken from early American architecture; they, in turn, hold that history and its inherent values. The house as a place of dwelling is a fundamental expression of individual freedom which is then extended to community out of need.[13]

It is the content of the works discussed as well as those in the exhibition that allows us to evaluate the architectural setting from an alternate perspective:

Now and in the past, most of the time the majority of people live by borrowed ideas and upon traditional accumulations, yet at every moment the fabric is being undone and a new one is woven to replace the old, while from time to time the whole pattern shakes and quivers, settling into new shapes and figures.[14]

And Gaston Bachelard writes:

For our house is our corner of the world. As has often been said it is our first universe, a real cosmos in every sense of the word. If we look at it inti-

mately, the humblest dwelling has beauty.

. . . all really inhabited space bears the essence of the notion of home . . . the sheltered being gives perceptible limits to his shelter. He experiences the house in reality, and is its virtuality, by means of thought and dreams. . . . The house, like fire and water . . . recall[s] flashes of daydreams that illuminate the synthesis of immemorial and recollected. . . .

. . . Thus, the house is not experienced from day to day only, on the thread of a narrative, or in the telling of our own story. Through dreams, the various dwelling-places in our lives co-penetrate and retain the treasures of former days.[15]

Dextra Frankel
April 1983

NOTES

1. Charmaine Locke, *The Image of the House in Contemporary Art, Exploring the Relationship of Art and Architecture to Society* (Houston: The Lawndale Annex of the University of Houston, 1981), n.p.
2. Locke, exhibition proposal, 1980, n.p.
3. David Gebhard, "Charles Moore: Architecture and the New Vernacular," *Artforum*, vol. 3, no. 8 (May 1965): 53.
4. Title of the exhibition is courtesy of "The House That Art Built" by Michael H. Smith from his essay written for the CSUF exhibition catalogue.
5. H.C. Westermann in *The Image of the House in Contemporary Art, Exploring the Relationship of Art and Architecture to Society*, by Charmaine Locke (Houston: The Lawndale Annex of the University of Houston, 1981), n.p.
6. Interview of Tony Berlant by Dextra Frankel, Santa Monica, April 21, 1983.
7. Ibid.
8. ibid.
9. Lecture by Roland Reiss, Santa Ana College, April 22, 1983.
10. Ibid.
11. Ibid.
12. *Webster's New Collegiate Dictionary*, 1977, s.v. "vernacular."
13. Julie Brown, *Siah Armajani* (Yonkers: The Hudson River Museum, 1981), n.p.
14. George Kubler, *The Shape of Time* (New Haven and London: Yale University Press, 1962), pp. 17–18.
15. Gaston Bachelard, *The Poetics of Space* (Boston: Beacon Press, 1969), pp. 4,5.

If I were asked to name the chief benefit of the house, I should say: the house shelters daydreaming, the house protects the dreamer, the house allows one to dream in peace. . . . Past, present and future give the house different dynamisms, which often interfere, at times opposing, at others, stimulating one another. In the life of a man, the house thrusts aside contingencies, its councils of continuity are unceasing. Without it, man would be a dispersed being. It maintains him through the storms of the heavens and through those of life. It is body and soul. It is the human being's first world. Before he is "cast into the world," as claimed by certain hasty metaphysics, man is laid in the cradle of the house. And always, in our daydreams the house is a large cradle. A concrete metaphysics cannot neglect this fact, this simple fact, all and more since this fact is a value, an important value, to which we return in our daydreaming. Being is already a value. Life begins well, it begins enclosed, protected, all warm in the bosom of the house.[1]

The making of such things is building. Its nature consists in this, that it corresponds to the character of these things. *They are locations that* allow spaces. This is why building, by virtue of constructing locations, is a founding and a joining of spaces. Because building produces locations, the joining of the spaces of these locations necessarily brings with it space, as *spatium* [Latin: a space or an interval] and as *extensio* [Latin: extension], into the thingly structure of buildings. But building never shapes pure "space" as a single entity. Neither directly or indirectly. Nevertheless, because it produces things as locations, building *receives the directive* for its erecting of locations. . . . . The edifices guard the fourfold. . . . They are things matics. Building puts up locations that make space and a site for the fourfold. From the simple oneness in which earth and sky, divinities and mortals belong together, building *receives the directive* for its erecting of locations . . . . The edifices guard the fourfold. . . . They are things that in their own way preserve the fourfold: to save the earth, to receive the sky, to await the divinities, to escort the mortals—this fourfold preserving is the simple nature, the presencing of a dwelling. In this way, then, do genuine buildings give form to the dwelling in its presencing and house this presence.[2]

5

BY JAN BUTTERFIELD

Discussing the hut as metaphor, Gaston Bachelard examines *Le Serviteur* by Henri Bachelin, and he says:

"He goes to the very bottom of the 'hut dream,' which is well-known to everyone who cherishes the legendary images of primitive houses. But in most hut dreams we hope to live elsewhere, far from the over-crowded house, far from city cares. We flee in thought in search of a real refuge . . . the root of the hut dream [is] in the house itself. He has only to give a few touches to the spectacle of the family sitting-room, only to listen to the stove roaring in the stillness, while an icy wind blows against the house, to know that at the house's center, in the circle of light shed by the lamp, he is living in the round house, the primitive hut of prehistoric man."
Gaston Bachelard, *The Poetics of Space* (Boston: Beacon Press, 1969), p. 31.

"—But when I saw the great Gaudi church in Barcelona, the great Sagrada Familia, the great ghose of a cathedral or rather great skeleton of a cathedral, then did I realize especially after seeing also the plans and models in the basement for those portions of the great cathedral not yet built and perhaps never to be build . . . the amazingly few but truly dedicated workmen still working under the burning inspiration of the sainted Catalan architect Antonio Gaudi, having seen all this I then realized what I had not realized before, what had escaped my notice these many years, that not only is less more but that *more is more too.* I swooned, under the impact of the ethical corollary."
Donald Barthelme, "Grandmother's House," *Sixty Stories* (New York: E.P. Dutton, 1982), p. 453.

At Mycenae I walked over the incandescent dead; at Epidaurus I felt a stillness so intense that for a fraction of a second I heard the great heart of the world beat and I understood the meaning of pain and sorrow; at Tiryns I stood in the shadow of the Cyclopean man and felt the blaze of that inner eye which has now become a sickly gland; at Argos the whole plain was a fiery mist in which I saw the ghosts of our own American Indians and greeted them in silence. I moved about in a detached way, my feet flooded with the earthly glow. I am at Corinth in a rose light, the sun battling the moon, the earth turning slowly with its fat ruins, wheeling in light like a water-wheel reflected in a still pond. I am at Arachova when the eagle soars from its nest and hangs poised above the boiling cauldron of earth, stunned by the brilliant pattern of colors which dress the heaving abyss. I am at Leonidion at sundown and behind the heavy pall of marsh vapor looms the dark portal of the Inferno where the shades of bats and snakes and lizards come to rest, and perhaps to pray. In each place I open a new vein of experience, a miner digging deeper into the earth, approaching the heart of the star which is not yet extinguished.
Henry Miller, *The Colossus of Maroussi* (New York: New Directions, 1941), p. 57.

Humankind's need for shelter is instinctual, such as the needs for food and procreation. Primitive peoples built structures in trees and made "nests" in caves in which to dwell. Survivors of plane wrecks first create shelter out of the parts, to protect themselves from the elements, then search for food and water. The hunter, lost, first finds shelter which he often must make, then decides upon which course to take.

Shelter is basic, primal, mandatory for existence—but it also defines and shapes our lives. An individual's shelter, the house, is an important symbolic edifice. Whether constructed roughly out of daub and wattle or in the more sophisticated international style vocabulary of concrete, glass and steel, the house is a metaphor for wholeness, shelter, security, as well as for providing shelter. It is often the first thing a child learns to draw. So strong is its symbolism that as children we all drew the same house with the same two windows with sashed curtains, a door, and the same peaked roof, regardless of whether we grew up in an apartment complex or a Bauhaus-inspired California edifice where the roof was flat. For all of us, there was a single, commonly agreed upon symbol that meant "house."

Through the ages past societies have been defined, examined and psycho-analyzed through their houses. One has only to think, for example, how much we know about the people of Pompeii as a result of the structures and the residential amenities left intact in the wake of the lava flow. It isn't only houses which fascinate, engage and pique our intellectual curiosity, it is the purposeful structures which have been built through the ages—structures utilized for religious ceremonies, secular meetings or for play. The consuming lure of

Stonehenge derives from its very enigma. What does it tell us about the peoples who built it? Who, first of all, were they? For what purpose were the stones intended? If the purpose was religious, what was the religion? If the purposes were astronomical, where did the information come from? As diverse as those two purposes seem at first to be, the best educated contemporary guesses place the function and purpose of Stonehenge someplace between the two. The generally held theory is that the purpose was both religious and astronomical, and that the two were intertwined. For all of their muteness and enigma, the stones themselves have a presence and exude a spirituality which, on a sensate level, is far more vocal than is written history. They are carriers of spirituality and information, much of which we have second-guessed as we have the purpose and function of many Greek structures, although in the latter case, classical scholars at least have suppositional texts for reference. In *Overlay*, Lucy Lippard notes:

> There is a mysterious, romantic element to wondering about the past, however critically one goes about it. The ancient sites and images are talismans, aids to memory, outlets for the imagination that can't be regulated, owned or manipulated like so much contemporary art because so little is or ever will be known about them. Unlike a towering skyscraper, a towering standing stone in the landscape seems not so much to dominate its surroundings as to sensuously coexist with them. It confirms the

6

human need to touch, to hold and to make, in relationship to natural forces and phenomena. Even if we as individuals are cut off from any communal belief system or collective work system, something seems to flow back to us through these places—which we see perhaps as symbols of lost symbols, apprehended but not specifically comprehended in our own socioreligious context.[3]

In order to have shelter, man must, essentially, build. The larger implications of shelter are those of dwelling, which in its sophisticated aspects separates man from the animals. Whether it involves the lashing together of twigs or the building of huts, lean-tos or teepees, or construction with wood, brick, stucco, concrete and steel, building involves a progressively sophisticated, evolutionary thought pattern, a sense of building—geometry and aesthetics coupled with that of need or use.

Shelter not only keeps man alive, it serves to define and shape the quality of his aliveness, a given with which philosophy has long grappled. Heidegger, in a Cartesian mode, stated essentially, "I am, therefore I must dwell":

> Spaces open up by the fact that they are let into the dwelling of man. To say that mortals *are* is to say that *in dwelling* they persist through spaces by virtue of their stay among things and locations. And only because mortals pervade, persist through, space by their very nature are they able to go through their spaces.[4]

And he continues:

> Man's relation to locations, and through locations to spaces inheres in his dwelling. The relationship between man and space is none other than dwelling, strictly thought and spoken.[5]

The terraces of the garden are held up to the sun, the sun falls full upon them, they are like a vessel slanted up, to catch the superb, heavy light. Within the walls we are remote, perfect, moving in heavy spring sunshine, under the bony avenue of vines. . . . We came to a great stone building that I had thought was a storehouse, for open-air storage, because the walls are open halfway up, showing the darkness inside and the corner pillar very white and square and distinct in front of it.

Entering carelessly into the dimness, I started, for at my feet was a great floor of water, clear and green in its obscurity, going down between the walls, a reservoir in the gloom. . . . It stank, slightly, with a raw smell. . . . Then we climbed into a great loft of leaves, ruddy brown, stored in a great bank under the roof, seeming to give off a little red heat, as they gave off the lovely perfume of the hills. We passed through, and stood at the foot of the lemon-house. The big, blind building rose high in the sunshine before us.

All summer long, upon the mountain slopes steep by the lake, stand the rows of naked pillars rising out of the green foliage like ruins of temples: white, square pillars of masonry, standing forlorn in their colonnades and squares, rising up the mountain-sides here and there, as if they remained from some great race that had once worshipped here. And still, in the winter, some are seen, standing away in lonely places where the sun streams full, grey rows of pillars rising out of a broken wall, tier above tier, naked to the sky, forsaken.

They are the lemon plantations, and the pillars are to support the heavy branches of the trees. . . .

D.H. Lawrence, *Twilight in Italy* (New York: Penguin Books, 1981), pp. 54, 55.

Great literature is replete with images of dwelling, of shelter and of place. From the primitive huts in DeFoe's *Robinson Crusoe* and J.D. Wyss' *Swiss Family Robinson*, to the sophistication of Proust's *Remembrance of Things Past*, there are powerful images of the shelter, the structure, the grand or bourgeois house and sometimes of a specific room in that house:

> Great images have both a history and a prehistory; they are always a blend of memory and legend . . . primal images, simple engravings are but so many invitations to start imagining again. They give us back areas of being, houses in which human beings' certainty of being is concentrated, and we have the impression that, by living in such images as these, images that are as stabilizing as these are, we could start a new

I have already described my habitation, which was a tent under the side of a rock, surrounded with a strong pale of posts and cables, but I might now rather call it a wall, for I raised a kind of wall up against it of turfs, about two foot thick on the outside, and after some time, I think it was a year and a half, I raised rafters from it leaning to the rock and thatched or covered it with boughs of trees and such things as I could get to keep out the rain, which I found at some times . . . very violent. . . . I had no room to turn myself; so I set myself to enlarge my cave and works farther into the earth, for it was a loose sandy rock, which yielded easily to the labor I bestowed on it; and so,

7

when I found I was pretty safe as to beasts of prey, I worked sideways to the right hand into the rock, and then turning to the right again, worked quite out, and made me a door to come out on the outside of my pale or fortification.
Daniel Defoe, *Robinson Crusoe* (New York: The Modern Library, 1948), pp. 74–75.

I consulted several things in my situation, which I found would be proper for me: first, health and fresh water, I just now mentioned; secondly, shelter from the heat of the sun; thirdly, security from ravenous creatures, whether men or beasts; fourthly, a view to the sea, that if God sent any ship in sight, I might not lose any advantage for my deliverance, of which I was not willing to banish all my expectation yet.

In search of a place proper for this I found a little plain on the side of a rising hill, whose front towards this little plain was steep as a house-side so that nothing could come down upon me from the top; on the side of this rock there was a hollow place worn a little way in like the entrance or door of a cave, but there was not really any cave, or way into the rock at all.

On the flat of the green, just before this hollow place, I resolved to pitch my tent. This plain was not above an hundred yards broad and about twice as long, and lay like a green before my door and at the end of it descended irregularly every way down into the low grounds by the seaside. It was on the north-northwest side of the hill, so that I was sheltered from the heat every day, till it came to a west and by south sun, or thereabouts, which in those countries is near the setting.

Before I set up my tent, I drew a half circle before the hollow place, which took in about ten yards in its semi-diameter from the rock and twenty yards in its diameter, from its beginning and ending.

In this half circle I pitched two rows of strong stakes, driving them into the ground till they stood very firm like piles, the biggest end being out of the ground about five foot and a half and sharpened on the top.
Daniel Defoe, *Robinson Crusoe* (New York: The Modern Library, 1948), p. 64.

These houses stand widely scattered on the long straight "damms"; they are red, with green or blue timbering, smothered by thick, heavy straw roofs, and seem to be pressed down into the earth by their massive, pelt-like burden. Many of them can scarcely be seen from the damms; they have drawn the trees across their faces as protection from the never-ceasing winds. Their windows flash through the thick foliage, like jealous eyes looking out from a dark mask. They stand there peacefully, the smoke from the hearth filling them completely and flowing out of the black depth of the door and oozing through the cracks in the roof. On cool days it hangs round about the house, repeating its shape in sizes as large again and ghostly-grey. Within, the whole is practically one room, a wide, long-shaped room, in which the smell and the warmth of the cattle unite with the acrid frumes of the open fire to make a strange twilight, in which it would be quite possible to lose one's bearings. This "Diele" widens out further back, there are windows on the right and on the left, and straight ahead are the bedrooms. They contain little furniture. A spacious table, several chairs, a corner-

life, a life that would be our own, that would belong to us in our very depths. When we look at images of this kind . . . we start musing on primitiveness restored, desired, and experiences through simple images, for example, an album of pictures of huts would constitute a textbook of simple exercises for the phenomenology of the imagination.[6]

With writers such as Rilke, Sartre, Blake, D.H. Lawrence, Virginia Woolf and Lawrence Durrell, we are aware of the sensate presence of those rooms or places as well; our experience of them is phenomenological, or, perhaps more accurately, the writer wishes our experience of them to be phenomenological and has so described them that we might, in our imagination, *sense* them as does he or she.

cupboard with some glass and ware, and the enclosed, large bed-compartments with sliding doors. In this bed-cupboard the children are born, the hours of death and the wedding nights are passed. There, into this last, narrow, windowless darkness life has withdrawn, ousted from every other place in the whole house by work.

Rainer Maria Rilke, *Where Silence Reigns* (New York: New Directions, 1978), pp. 19–20.

Here is the Saint-Elémir tramway, I turn round and the objects turn with me, pale and green as oysters. . . . Bluish objects pass the windows. In jerks all stiff and brittle; people, walls; a house offers me its black heart through open windows; and the windows pale, all that is black becomes blue, blue this great yellow brick house advancing uncertainly, trembling, suddenly stopping and taking a nose dive. A man gets on and sits down opposite to me. The yellow house starts up again, it leaps against the windows, it is so close that you can only see part of it, it is obscured. The windows rattle. It rises, crushing, higher than you can see, with hundreds of windows opened on black hearts; it slides along the car brushing past it; night has come between the rattling windows. It slides interminably, yellow as mud, and the windows are sky blue. Suddenly it is no longer there, it has stayed behind, a sharp, grey illumination fills the car and spreads everywhere with inexorable justice: it is the sky; through the windows you can still see layer on layer of sky.

Jean Paul Sartre, *Nausea* (New York: New Directions, 1964), pp. 124–125.

Sometimes (with D.H. Lawrence) it is the exquisite sense of lemon gardens which shapes a place for us; at other times (with Durrell) it is the perfumed experience of a mauve dusk turned suddenly midnight blue, or (with Sartre) it is the unpleasantly dizzying, nauseating sense of *being* overlaid on *place* which transports us from one reality to another, so that we bring both self and memory response to the fore when we shape an image. Carl Jung has written of his tower, Virginia Wolfe of her room, Melville of an inn, Blake of a tent, Proust of a "nest," and in each case that which they have built for us is an aspect of the psyche or the self. Through these structures symbolically, we are privy by metaphor to the unconscious of another.

I used to sit and write in the great loft of the lemon-house, high up, far, far from the ground, the open front giving across the lake and the mountain snow opposite, flush with twilight. The old matting and boards, the old disused implements of lemon culture made shadows in the deserted place. Then there would come the call from the back, away above: *"Venga, venga mangiare."*

We ate in the kitchen, where the olive and laurel wood burned in the open fireplace. It was always soup in the evening. Then we played games or cards, all playing; or there was singing, with the accordion, and sometimes a rough mountain peasant with a guitar.

D.H. Lawrence, *Twilight in Italy* (New York: Penguin Books, 1981), pp. 102–103.

It was the best hour of the day in Alexandria—the streets turning slowly to the metallic blue of carbon paper but still giving off the heat of the sun. Not all the lights were on in the town, and the large mauve parcels of dusk moved here and there, blurring the outlines of everything, repainting the hard outlines of buildings and human beings in smoke.

Lawrence Durrell, *Mountolive* (New York: E.P. Dutton, 1958), p. 143.

Things are bad! Things are very bad: I have it, the filth, the Nausea. And this time it is new: it caught me in a café. Until now cafes were my only refuge because they were full of people and well lighted: now there won't even be that any more; when I am run to earth in my room, I shan't know where to go.... I was surrounded, seized by a slow, coloured mist, and a whirlpool of lights in the smoke, in the mirrors, in the booths glowing at the back of the cafe, and I couldn't see why it was there or why it was like that. I was on the doorstep, I hesitated to go in and then there was a whirlpool, an eddy, a shadow passed across the ceiling and I felt myself pushed forward. I floated, dazed by luminous fogs dragging me in all directions at once.... I wanted to vomit. And since that time, the Nausea has not left me, it holds me.

... [a] blue cotton shirt stands out joyfully against a chocolate-coloured wall. That too brings on the Nausea. The Nausea is not inside me: I feel it *out there* in the wall, in the suspenders, everywhere around me. It makes itself one with the cafe. I am the one who is within *it*.

Jean Paul Sartre, *Nausea* (New York: New Directions, 1964), pp. 18–19.

Gradually, through my scientific work, I was able to put my fantasies and the contents of the unconscious on a solid footing. Words and paper, however, did not seem real enough to me; something more was needed. I had to achieve a kind of representation in stone of my innermost thoughts and of the knowledge I had acquired. Or, to put it another way, I had to make a confession of faith in stone. That was the beginning of the "Tower," the house which I built for myself at Bollingen.... At first I did not plan a proper house, but merely a kind of primitive one-story dwelling. It was to be a round structure with a hearth in the center and bunks along the walls. I more or less had in mind an African hut where the fire, ringed by a few stones, burns in the middle, and the whole life of the family revolves around this center. Primitive huts concretize an idea of wholeness, a familial wholeness in which all sorts of small domestic animals likewise participate.

C.G. Jung, *Memories, Dreams, Reflections* (New York: Vintage Books, 1973), p. 223.

The division in our life was curious. Downstairs there was pure convention: upstairs pure intellect.

... the pressure of society in 1900 almost forbade any natural feeling. Perhaps I was too young. Perhaps I was wrongly adjusted. At any rate I never met a man or a woman with whom I struck up any real relationship. All the same there was the excitement of clothes, of lights, of society, in short; and the queerness, the strangeness of being alone, on my own, for a moment, with some complete stranger: he in white waistcoat and gloves, I in white satin and gloves. A more unreal relationship cannot be imagined; but there was a thrill in the unreality. For when I was once more in my own room I would see it small and untidy: I would ride the waves of the party still: I would lie in bed, tossing up and down on the things I had said, heard and done. And next morning I would still be thinking, as I read my Sophocles, of the party.

Virginia Woolf, *A Sketch of the Past* (New York: Harcourt Brace Jovanovich, 1976), p. 134.

Entering that gable-ended Spouter-Inn, you found yourself in a wide, low, straggling entry with old-fashioned wainscots, reminding one of the bulwarks of some condemned old craft. On one side hung a very large oil-painting so thoroughly besmoked, and every way defaced, that in the unequal cross-lights by which you viewed it, it was only by diligent study and a series of systematic visits to it, and careful inquiry of the neighbors, that you could any way arrive at an understanding of its purpose. Such unaccountable masses of shades and shadows, that at first you almost thought some ambitious young artist, in the time of the New England hags, had endeavored to delineate chaos bewitched. But by dint of much and earnest contemplation, and oft repeated ponderings, and especially by throwing open the little window towards the back of the entry, you at last come to the conclusion that such an idea, however wild, might not be altogether unwarranted.

But what most puzzled and confounded you was a long, limber, portentous, black mass of something hovering in the centre of the picture over three blue, dim, perpendicular lines floating in a nameless yeast. A boggy, soggy, squitchy picture truly, enough to drive a nervous man distracted. Yet was there a sort of indefinite, half-attained, unimaginable sublimity about it that fairly froze you to it, till you involuntarily took an oath with yourself to find out what that marvellous painting meant. Ever and anon a bright, but, alas, deceptive idea would dart you through.—It's the Black Sea in a midnight gale.—It's the unnatural combat of the four primal elements.—It's a blasted heath. —It's a Hyperborean winter scene.—It's the breaking-up of the ice-bound stream of Time. But at last all these fancies yielded to that one portentous something in the picture's midst. *That* once found out, and all the rest were plain. But stop; does it not bear a faint resemblance to a gigantic fish? even the great leviathan himself?

Herman Melville, *Moby Dick* (Chicago: The Great Books Foundation, 1956), pp. 13–14.

I had seen first one and then another of the rooms in which I had slept during my life, and in the end I would revisit them all in the long course of my waking dream: rooms in winter, where on going to bed I would at once bury my head in a nest, built up out of the most diverse materials, the corner of my pillow, the top of my blankets, a piece of a shawl, the edge of my bed, and a copy of an evening paper, all of which things I would contrive, with the infinite patience of birds building their nests, to cement into one whole; rooms where, in a keen frost, I would feel the satisfaction of being shut in from the outer world (like the sea-swallow which builds at the end of a dark tunnel and is kept warm by the surrounding earth), and where, the fire keeping in all night, I would sleep wrapped up, as it were, in a great cloak of snug and savoury air, shot with the glow of the logs which would break out again in flame: in a sort of alcove without walls, a cave of warmth dug out of the heart of the room itself, a zone of heat whose boundaries were constantly shifting and altering in temperature as gusts of air ran across them to strike freshly upon my face, from the corners of the room, or from parts near the window or far from the fireplace which had therefore remained cold.

Marcel Proust, *Swann's Way* (New York: Vintage Books, 1970), p. 6.

11. "Spread a Tent with strong curtains around them
Let cords & states bind in the Void
That Eternals may no more behold them."
12. They began to weave curtains of darkness;
They erected large pillars round the Void,
With golden hooks fasten'd in the pillars.
With infinite labour the Eternals
William Blake, *The Book of Urizen* (New York: Random House, 1978), p. 56.

In 1972, a new compound, known as the Whites, or the New York Five, made its bid. . . . the five being Peter Eisenman, Michael Graves, John Hejduk, Richard Meier, and Charles Gwathmey. . . . The work of the Whites you could tell at a glance. Their buildings were white . . . and baffling. They could barely stand to introduce the occasional black or gray touch, such as the band of black painted at the base of a wall to do the work of the old (bourgeois) baseboards. They were convinced that the way to be nonbourgeois, in the new age, was to be scrupulously pure, as Corbu had been scrupulously pure, and to be baffling.
Tom Wolfe, *From Bauhaus to Our House* (New York: Farrar Straus Giroux, 1981), p. 120. .

For example, in addition to a house in Princeton, [Michael Graves] created a post-and-beam projection that looked like a David Smith sculpture adapted by Rietveld—and painted it blue. This was supposed to *resonate* with the familiar middle-middle blue sky overhead as one walked under it. Whether anybody actually got that or not was not nearly so important as recognizing the sophistication of the approach. Later, Graves edged toward Moore's position of playing Classical forms, notably columns, against modern facades so thin that, quite deliberately, they had the look of cardboard. The results resembled the backdrops in the typical resort community production of *Aïda*.
Tom Wolfe, *From Bauhaus to Our House* (New York: Farrar Straus Giroux, 1981), p. 138.

It is a great distance from the earliest art which concerned itself with architecture (extremely early if one thinks of the undulating projecting walls of the Lascaux caves upon whose surfaces cave dwellers drew magical horses and bison). One thinks, for example, of the architectural thrones erected to shelter the Madonna in the paintings of Giotto and Cimabue, of great sculptural works such as the figures on the tympanum at Autun, the figures on the exterior of the Chartres cathedral and the bronze doors of Ghiberti. The remarkable Gothic frame created by van Eyck for the Ghent altarpiece is another classic example of the recognition and incorporation of architecture within the framework of art.

By the same token, architecture has come a long way from its earliest vernacular beginnings in the primitive hut, to the refined, disciplined spaces of contemporary architecture. Although humans have been building with great creativity for thousands of years, the *history* of architecture has concerned itself only with the last few hundred. In addition, it has been only in the 1980s that architecture has been mentioned in the same breath as art.

One of the most overt examples is the exhibition, "Houses for Sale," held at Leo Castelli's gallery at the beginning of the 1980s. Castelli Gallery, which set the measure for so much of what in the sixties and seventies was regarded as "hard art" or "blue chip" art, now took the lead in an entirely new area: architecture. The much heralded exhibition included the work of eight architects (Emilio Ambasz, Peter Eisenman, Vittorio Gregotti, Arata Isozaki, Charles Moore, Cesar Pelli, Cedric Price and Oswald Mathias Ungers) as objects for outright sale, on the open market. These houses were created totally at the creative and aesthetic whim of the architect, to be sold to the collector unchanged, as are paintings and sculpture.

Another prominent dealer, Max Protetch, whose gallery came into being in the 1970s, early on began showing drawings of the work of architects such as those of the "New York Five" (Richard Meier, Charles Gwathmey, John Hedjuk, Peter Eisenman and Michael Graves). Interestingly, we find ourselves at a point in time when it is possible to purchase a Michael Graves architectural rendering as a drawing, or to commission an Arata Isozaki house—complete—as a work of art. In Los Angeles, Isozaki, receiving input from major artists, has designed a bold, space-sensitive edifice to house works of art. This structure will become the permanent home of the Los Angeles Museum of Contemporary Art. Some interesting lines have been crossed, some important roles redefined. And the concept of shelter has been greatly extended.

To give an example: one of the contemporary visionary architects whose works best exemplify the merger of art and architecture is the remarkable Luis Barragan, the Mexican architect whose work was known in this country only to a few initiates, until recently. Then in 1976, New York's Museum of Modern Art presented an exhibition of his work, creating enormous ripples in the worlds of both art and architecture. "I don't know who this guy is," artist Robert Irwin said, "but he's one of us."

In 1980, Barragan, who has now passed his eightieth birthday, received the coveted Pritzker Prize for architecture—the architectural equivalent of the Nobel Prize. This relatively unknown artist/architect, whose houses are a passionate emotional statement reflecting his personal philosophy, finally achieved international recognition. Writing about his work, Barragan speaks more like a painter than an architect:

> My house is my refuge, an emotional piece of architecture. . . . I believe in an "emotional architecture." It is very important for humankind that architecture should move by its beauty; if there are many equally valid technical solutions to a problem, the one which offers the user a message of beauty and emotion, that one is architecture.[7]

Barragan's work is an impeccable meeting of right angles and an exquisite sense of contrasting textures: Spanish tile against rough stucco, enormous natural rock formations paired off against solemn vertical slatted gates. Everywhere there is cooling water and brilliant color. It is not simply the forms which please, but the serenely hedonistic use of color, the kind of color not previously seen in architecture: here a spill of midnight black water rippling on a flattened ground plan shoots like a geometric river through a grove of Eucalyptus trees and stops at a door of brilliant blue hidden in their midst; there a freestanding wall of vermilion stucco pulsates powerfully in the sun; there a wall of warm plum abuts a ground cover of smoothed pebbles which swoops downward to a shallow pool. The stunning directness of this work is fleshed out in a myriad of sensate ways. The intense shimmering Mexican heat is everywhere, heightened by the dancing reflections of water which break up some of the rectangular surfaces and a much welcomed breeze occasionally stirring leaves of the enormous Eucalyptus trees.

It is in works such as these that one can clearly see art and architecture merge —in these contemporary structures, the dignity of whose upright walls and stones seems to recall the inherent rightness of Stonehenge, and whose heightened sense of place incorporates the Greek concept of *Peras*. Martin Heidegger said of *Peras* that—

> A space is something that has been made room for, something that is cleared and free, namely within a boundary, *Peras* [Greek: boundary]. A boundary is not that at which something stops but, as the Greeks recognized, *the boundary is that from which something begins its presencing*. . . . Accordingly, spaces receive their being from location and not from "space."[8]

Writing at the time of the Pritzker Prize, Paul Goldberger from *The New York Times* news service said:

> Barragan is different. Few imitate his works directly. But his quest to express a certain spirit of serenity, a sense of warmth and repose and dignity, has been admired by architects around the world. For his forms, while highly personal, do connect closely with the larger currents of architectural thought today. Barragan's work is deceptively simple. His projects generally consist of basic elements such as walls, pools, fountains and gardens, *all arranged in an abstract and almost mystical fashion.*[9]

In the last decade and a half there has been a great hue and cry in the art world about the death of Formalism, which had essentially allowed only line, form, shape and color as proper elements for consideration when examining the relative merits of a work of art. The Formalist theory insisted on the implication of flatness of surface (which never made much sense) and that the work be holistic in its gestalt—tidy but tedious. Unbelievably, this theory offered no room for content, yet content would seem to be a kind of imperative for art. As Albert Elsen noted in the introduction to his book, *The Purposes of Art*:

> To ignore content is to distort the exciting record of how through art men have reacted to the world and the self. Content must be seen in relation to purpose and to style. The whole art object benefits from being set into the context of even a small part of its originating environment and the continuity of problems and possibilities that have concerned artists over long periods of time. Art is thus more than visual experience, providing rich intellectual and emotional rewards, for it is not philosophy alone that has the capacity to demonstrate the polyphonic unity of culture.[10]

As far as Formalism was concerned, rigor mortis had set in long before its death. With its death, a further mandate was rendered null and void—a mandate which dictated that art be a portable, purchasable consumer product, and that it be an "object." In the 1970s, a whole generation of artists emerged who began, in various ways, to tap prehistory, history and vernacular "built" structures for form and content in relation to sources for their own art. As Lucy Lippard notes—

> While American artists in the '40s and '50s arrived at mythological

It will be understood that the latter are artists: poets or painters, composers or architects, fundamentally lonely spirits, who, in turning to Nature, put the eternal above the transitory, that which is most profoundly based on law above that which is fundamentally ephemeral, and who, since they cannot persuade Nature to concern herself with them, see their task to be the understanding of Nature, so that they may take their place somewhere in her great design. And the whole of humanity comes nearer to Nature in these isolated and lonely ones. It is not the least and is, perhaps, the peculiar value of art, that it is the medium in which man and landscape, form and world, meet and find one another.
Rainer Maria Rilke, *Where Silence Reigns* (New York: New Directions, 1978), p. 9.

13

themes primarily via classical sources, today's vernacular tends to be less interested in classical periods and has been primarily attracted by the archaic and prehistoric. These artists are rebelling against reductive purism and an art-for-art's sake emphasis on form or image alone with a gradual upsurge of mythical and ritual concept related to nature and to the origins of social life. Paralleled by a fascination with the subtly simple forms of pre-Classical architecture and by the development of the "fetishistic object."[11]

There was little mourning when Formalism died, not so much really as a wake. In fact, in some quarters there were celebrations and joy in the streets. Suddenly narration, content, politics, feminism, figuration and emotion flooded the art arena, along with a reinvestigation of the primitive, a deep concern with architectural structures and with site-determined works. An amazing amount of work took the shape of huts, kivas, tombs, rooms, spaces, mazes, barriers, places and houses. For the first time in memory these architecturally created or "built" structures did not relate to the overtly or covertly anthropomorphic structures of old, nor to Constructivism. Instead of being aloof from humankind, these new structures were *defined* by human beings and human presence. They afforded a place to dwell, if only metaphorically. By the same token there was a new concern for phenomenology, stemming from the belief that man defines his universe, which solipsistic belief is indeed true from an immediate, sensate perspective:

> Trekking across the vast, undulating, deceptively featureless landscape of the English moore—depending as much on intuition as on map and compass—sighting a distant silhouette against the sky (sheep? the promised stone circle?), or coming suddenly upon a single standing stone, I was glad there were no markers, no car parks, no brochures, glad to maintain a sense of discovery. The unpeopled megalithic sites and earth monuments, like more recently abandoned ruins, bring us back to art in an unself-conscious context. Freedom from my own daily space opened up new views of history. I began to perceive places as spatial metaphors for temporal distance. Such a dialectic is a major part of the Stones' attraction. They offer a framework within which to explore the crucial connections between individual desires (to make something, to hold something) and the social values that determine what we make and why.[12]

In the 1980s, as attitudes regarding art and architecture come closer, the "what we make and why," among painters and sculptors alike, seems frequently to relate to space and place and/or to take form as a built structure. Thus, as architecture, in the throes of its post-Modernist phase, has become more like art (forsaking many aspects of the work and teachings of the three great masters: Mies van der Rohe, Le Corbusier and Frank Lloyd Wright, and seeking less purity, newly erratic form and eclectic embellishment), one aspect of *visual art* in its post-Modernist or, if you will, post-Formalist phase, has become more like architecture.

Contemporarily and generationally, the historical antecedents for much of this new, "walk-in" art work are artists who came to the fore in the 1960s, such as Edward Kienholz and George Segal. Kienholz' existential, life-sized tableaux deal with birth, death, sexuality and temporality. They force us to examine the shadow side of our psyches. Segal's symbolic yet enigmatic "set pieces" serve as a frame of reference for his white figures made of bronze or plaster, which are eloquent in their muteness. The fact that both Kienholz and Segal cast from life is a highly relevant factor both in relation to the capacity of the figures to carry the work's implicit message and to "Be"—in the houses built for them.

The term "house" in this exhibition is meant to include "places" or "spaces" of many kinds. The only links or qualities of "akinness" among the artists in the exhibition are those of implied literalness and/or the manner in which they make manifest an experiential or phenomenological experience as opposed,

Every new $900,000 summer house in the north woods of Michigan or on the shore of Long Island has so many pipe railings, ramps, hob-tread metal spiral stairways, sheets of industrial plate glass, banks of tungsten-halogen lamps, and white cylindrical shapes, it looks like an insecticide refinery. I once saw the owners of such a place driven to the edge of sensory deprivation by the whiteness & lightness & leanness & cleanness & bareness & spareness of it all. They became desperate for an antidote, such as coziness & color. They tried to bury the obligatory white sofas under Thai-silk throw pillows of every rebellious, iridescent shade of magenta, pink and tropical green imaginable. But the architect returned, as he always does, like the conscience of a Calvinist, and he lectured them and hectored them and shucked the shimmering little sweet things out.

Tom Wolfe, *From Bauhaus to Our House* (New York: Farrar Straus Giroux, 1981), pp. 3, 4.

14

say, to the apprehension of an *object*, which is the case with work of artists such as Anthony Caro, Don Judd, Richard Serra and Sol Lewitt. At the same time, artists in this exhibition have a great deal in common with artists such as Robert Irwin, Robert Smithson, Christo and Michael Heizer, none of whom are included in this presentation because, for all intents and purposes, they do not build "houses" or structures in the true connotated sense of those terms. All, however, are acutely involved with a sense of place.

I would be lying stretched out on my bed, a book in my hand, in my room which trembled with the effort to defend its frail, transparent coolness against the afternoon sun, behind its almost closed shutters through which, however, a reflection of the sunlight had contrived to slip in on its golden wings, remaining motionless, between glass and woodwork, in a corner, like a butterfly poised upon a flower.

This dim freshness of my room was to the broad daylight of the street what the shadow is to the sunbeam, that is to say, equally luminous, and presented to my imagination the entire panorama of summer.

Marcel Proust, *Swann's Way* (New York: Vintage Books, 1970), pp. 62–63.

The Casa di Paoli is quite a splendid place. It is large, pink and cream, rising up to a square tower in the centre, throwing off a painted loggia at either extreme of the façade. It stands a little way back from the road, just above the lake, and grass grows on the bay of cobbled pavement in front. When at night the moon shines full on this pale facade, the theatre is far outdone in staginess.

The hall is spacious and beautiful, with great glass doors at either end, through which shine the courtyards where bamboos fray the sunlight and geraniums glare red. The floor is of soft red tiles, oiled and polished like glass, the walls are washed grey-white, the ceiling is painted with pink roses and birds.

This is half-way between the outer world and the interior world, it partakes of both.

The other rooms are dark and ugly. There is no mistake about their being interior. They are like furnished vaults. The red-tiled, polished floor in the drawing-room seems cold and clammy, the carved, cold furniture stands in its tomb, the air has been darkened and starved to death, it is perished.

D.H. Lawrence, *Twilight in Italy* (New York: Penguin Books, 1981), pp. 40–41.

And so at last, following the curves of the green embankments you come upon an old house built sideways upon an intersection of violet canals, its cracked and faded shutters tightly fastened, its rooms hung with dervish trophies, hide shields, bloodstained spears and magnificent carpets. The gardens desolate and untended. Only the little figures on the wall move their celluloid wings—scarecrows which guard against the Evil Eye. The silence of complete desuetude. But then the whole countryside of Egypt shares this melancholy feeling of having been abandoned, allowed to run to seed, to bake and crack and moulder under the brazen sun.

Lawrence Durrell, *Clea* (New York: Pocket Books, 1960), p. 39.

Breadalby was a Georgian house with Corinthian pillars, standing among the softer, greener hills of Derbyshire, not far from Cromford. In front, it looked over a lawn, over a few trees, down to a string of fish-ponds in the hollow of the silent park. At the back were trees, among which were to be found the stables, and the big kitchen garden, behind which was a wood.

It was a very quiet place, some miles from the high-road, back from the Derwent Valley, outside the show scenery. Silent and forsaken, the golden stucco showed between the trees, the house-front looked down the park, unchanged and unchanging. . . . The summer was just coming in when Ursula and Gudrun went to stay the second time with Hermione. Coming along in the car, after they had entered the park, they looked across the dip, where the fish-ponds lay in silence, at the pillared front of the house, sunny and small like an English drawing of the old school, on the brow of the green hill, against the trees. There were small figures on the green lawn, women in lavender and yellow moving to the shade of the enormous, beautifully balanced cedar tree.

"Isn't it complete!" said Gudrun. "It is as final as an old aquatint."

D.H. Lawrence, *Sons and Lovers* (New York: Octopus/Heinemann, 1979), p. 685.

Every morning I pace
My pit like a bear
Turn turn again turn
Sky glitters like a chain
Every morning I pace
My pit like a bear
In the cell next to mine
Water is running
The jailer clinks his keys
As he comes and goes
In the cell next to mine
Water is running

Guillaume Apollinaire, *Alcools* (Berkeley: University of California Press, 1965), p. 189.

It was a tall room, so tall that it was roofed by darkness, despite the yellow flapping of the match-flame; one huge shattered window faintly reflected starlight. The walls were of verdigris, the plaster peeling everywhere, and their only decoration was the imprint of little blue hands which ran round the four walls in a haphazard pattern. As if a lot of pygmies had gone mad with blue paint and then galloped all over the walls standing on their hands!

Lawrence Durrell, *Clea* (New York: Pocket Books, 1960), pp. 138–139.

. . . the great panels of the brass-framed windows in the Yacht Club blazed like diamonds, throwing a brilliant light upon the snowy tables with their food, setting fire to the glasses and jewellery and eyes in a last uneasy conflagration before the heavy curtains would be drawn and the faces which had gathered . . . took on the warm pallors of candlelight.

Lawrence Durrell, *Balthazar* (New York: E.P. Dutton, 1961), p. 45.

It was a queer sort of place—a gable-ended old house, one side palsied as it were, and leaning over sadly. It stood on a sharp bleak corner, where that tempestuous wind Euroclydon kept up a worse howling than ever it did about poor Paul's tossed craft. Euroclydon, nevertheless, is a mighty pleasant zephyr to any one in-doors, with his feet on the hob quietly toasting for bed. "In judging of that tempestuous wind called Euroclydon," says an old writer—of whose works I possess the only copy extant— "it maketh a marvellous difference, whether thou lookest out at it from a glass window where the frost is all on the outside, or whether thou observest it from that sashless window, where the frost is on both sides, and of which the wight Death is the only glazier."

Herman Melville, *Moby Dick* (Chicago: The Great Books Foundation, 1956), p. 12.

16

. . . —or rooms in summer, where I would delight to feel myself a part of the warm evening, where the moonlight striking upon the half-opened shutters would throw down to the foot of my bed its enchanted ladder; where I would fall asleep, as it might be in the open air, like a titmouse which the breeze keeps poised in the focus of a sunbeam—or sometimes the Louis XVI room, so cheerful that I could never feel really unhappy, even on my first night in it: that room where the slender columns which lightly supported its ceiling would part, ever so gracefully, to indicate where the bed was and to keep it separate; sometimes again that little room with the high ceiling, hollowed in the form of a pyramid out of two separate storeys, and partly walled with mahogany, in which from the first moment my mind was drugged by the unfamiliar scent of flowering grasses, convinced of the hostility of the violet curtains and of the insolent indifference of a clock that chattered on at the top of its voice as though I were not there; while a strange and pitiless mirror with square feet, which stood across one corner of the room, cleared for itself a site I had not looked to find tenanted in the quiet surroundings of my normal field of vision: that room in which my mind, forcing itself for hours on end to leave its moorings, to elongate itself upwards so as to take on the exact shape of the room, and to reach to the summit of that monstrous funnel, had passed so many anxious nights while my body lay stretched out in bed, my eyes staring upwards, my ears straining, my nostrils sniffing uneasily, and my heart beating. . . .

Rainer Maria Rilke, *Where Silence Reigns* (New York: New Directions, 1978), p. 6.

. . . I ran up to the top of the house to cry by myself in a little room beside the schoolroom and beneath the roof, which smelt of orris-root, and was scented also by a wild currant-bush which had climbed up between the stones of the outer wall and thrust a flowering branch in through the half-opened window. Intended for a more special and a baser use, this room, from which, in the daytime, I could see as far as the keep of Roussainville-le-Pin, was for a long time my place of refuge, doubtless because it was the only room whose door I was allowed to lock, whenever my occupation was such as required an inviolable solitude; reading or dreaming, secret tears or paroxysms of desire.

Marcel Proust, *Swann's Way* (New York: Vintage Books, 1970), p. 10.

But to fix my mind upon the nursery—it had a balcony; there was a partition, but it joined the balcony of my father's and mother's bedroom. My mother would come out onto her balcony in a white dressing gown. There were passion flowers growing on the wall; they were great starry blossoms, with purple streaks, and large green buds, part empty, part full.

If I were a painter I should paint these first impressions in pale yellow, silver, and green. There was the pale yellow blind; the green sea; and the silver of the passion flowers. I should make a picture that was globular; semi-transparent; I should make curved shapes, showing the light through, but not giving a clear outline. Everything would be large and dim; and what was seen would at the same time be heard; sounds would come through this petal or leaf—sounds indistinguishable from sights.

The strength of these pictures—but sight was always then so much mixed with sound that picture is not the right word—the strength anyhow of these impressions makes me again digress. Those moments—in the nursery, on the road to the beach—can still be more real than the present moment.

Virginia Woolf, *Moments of Being* (New York: Harcourt Brace Jovanovich, 1976), pp. 66–67.

The exquisite room-environment pieces created by Robert Irwin in the 1970s had phenomenological, sensate presence, an ephemeral existence the experience of which is almost entirely in the eye/mind of the beholder. Irwin's pieces are always site-defined; that is, it is the site itself that "shapes" the pieces, and in that sense they are not "built," with the exception of an occasional premise of a wall. His primary materials for a decade and a half have consisted almost entirely of sunlight, shadow, string or scrim.

By the same token, Robert Smithson's important "Spiral Jetty" and his equally elegant "Broken Circle" and "Spiral Hill" manifest a deep knowledge of and concern for nature and for entropy, and an impeccable sense of place. But while created, sculpted out of the land, they were not "built" in the sense that rooms and houses are built. Equally, Michael Heizer's earthworks and christo's wrapped pieces and curtains, such as "Valley Curtain" and "Running Fence" and the "Surrounded Islands, Biscayne Bay, Greater Miami, Florida" belong to this *other* branch of experiential works which are concerned very much with "place"—*in situ*. While all may choose to alter that place, they do not essentially build upon it (yet as soon as one tries to generalize, there are exceptions, as evidenced in the "built" quality of Heizer's "Complex One/The City").

As we reach the mid-'80s, a new group of artists has become on one hand more narrative, more literal than either Segal or Kienholz, and on the other, virtually as phenomenological or experiential as Irwin, Smithson, Heizer and Christo, yet within a context of *fabricated* space. In Roland Reiss' "stage sets," in either doll-house size or in human scale, there is a quality of abstraction (particularly in the walk-in ones made of neutral, unpainted particle board or Formica) and of narration (in his diminutive works replete with mini-detective story clues). The same thing is true of Michael McMillen's perfectly created "H.O. gauge" worlds or of the pseudo-archeological presentations of Richard Turner and Bruce Williams, which evoke a sense of the mystery and adventure of other places, other cultures and earlier times. In the works of all these artists we find a strong literal and metaphorical involvement with the house or building as symbol, as a miniature stage on which the viewer can play out his or her own metaphysical journeys.

Another artist with whom we are concerned is Tony Berlant, whose archetypical little houses executed "sculpture pedestal" size, and his larger, more complex human scale ones are just as poignant as those we drew as children. They are simple, stylized, with two windows and a door, and many are executed with a child's sense of color, here applied with Berlant's unique neo-primitive metal collage which overlays parts of a world globe upon a tiny house, for example, layering it metaphorically and expanding the implications of its existence.

Donna Dennis' houses and facades are also symbolic, but in addition they are much more overtly representational. In Berlant's houses—which are also boxes of a sort—*contents matter*. One small house contains a huge conch shell, which, like the apple in Magritte's "Listening Room," has phenomenologically filled the entire space. Donna Dennis' houses, whether created in three-dimensional or in faux movie or stage flat style, are impenetrable. Whether subway facades or ubiquitous midwestern screenporch frame houses, they glow from within, yet their windows and portals are shaded, their contents remaining forever an enigma. Vija Celmins' small sealed houses, created early in her career, are also basic house structures, yet her houses are virtually incorporeal—their physical presence denied, obscured by exteriors upon which are painted blue skies and clouds, or smoke and flames.

18

At the other end of the scale, the "houses" of Siah Armajani are sophisticated architectural structures designed for use, often created with simple, rough materials. An example is "Reading Room" created for Baxter Art Gallery, incorporating Robert Frost's poetry stenciled about the walls, and within whose structure poets gave readings. Another, "Newstand," created for the Contemporary Arts Center in Cincinnati, also was meant to be physically entered, used. As much about theory, experience and social function as they are about aesthetics and "built" structures, Armajani's works can be experienced on a multiplicity of levels.

Predicated upon an entirely different point of view which places the emphasis on the experiential/alchemical qualities of the piece, rather than on its "building" or its real physical structure, Eric Orr creates magical rooms. Two of the most notable of these were "Silence and the Ion Wind," created for the Los Angeles County Museum of Art, in which inky, ion-filled blackness led to a gold-leafed chamber opening onto another world, or "Sunrise," built into his studio. This latter piece was a solemn, silent chamber built of lead the color of silvered moth's wings, and carpeted to screen out the noise of the world beyond its parameters; it tracked the sun, dragging its rays slowly down one wall in a luminous golden bar.

There are a number of artists included in "The House That Art Built" who create constructed spaces, rooms, enclosures, tombs, kivas, huts and so forth in which the experience of the space is paramount, yet whose physical attributes are often quite handsome in and of themselves. One thinks, for example, of the metaphysical chambers, structures and "machines" created by Alice Aycock, which fill whole rooms and which, in the beginning, had complex literary associations. Aycock mentions "Piranesi's prison architecture, the Egyptian *Book of the Dead* and Italo Calvino's *Invisible Cities* among her extensive sources (sharing this strong literary affiliation with Richard Turner and Bruce Williams whose sources are Robbe-Grillet and Yukio Mishima). Aycock's beautifully built infernal machines or fantastic constructions of raw, unpainted wood are unique in their merger of object with experience. They share by symbiosis many common traits with the new work of Robert Oppenheim who, like others we have just discussed, also does not build *houses*.

The outdoor structures of Mary Miss, such as "Sunken Pool," provided the sensation of being removed from reality and enclosed in a private world. In this opaquely turquoise structure which rose off the land and was framed by clean, unpainted two-by-fours, one found water, and as one descended (or *if*), one saw only sky. Other vernacular underground pieces by Mary Miss have their roots in American Indian dwellings, in the beehive tombs of Mycenea and in a multitude of other primitive sources. The works of Miss and others such as Richard Fleischner, Robert Stackhouse, Harriet Feigenbaum and even Jon Peterson have their roots in what Bernard Rudofsky called "architecture without architects," or what he terms "nonpedigreed architecture." Rudofsky also terms this "vernacular, anonymous, spontaneous, indigenous and rural architecture." He notes, "It is often architecture by subtraction or sculpted architecture" (carved out of rocks and caves, for example). Here one can see where possible roots for Smithson and Heizer may lie as well. In Rudofsky's remarkable book he discusses everything from the amphitheaters of Muyy-uray (halfway between Cuzco and Machu Picchu) which seem to have served as inspiration for a large number of earthwork artists (Robert Morris, Beverly Pepper, Herbert Bayer, to name but a few) to an underground village near Loyang in northern China, to churches in Abyssinia hewn out of stone, to a two dozen or more variants on hillside town dwellings and two dozen more variants of lacy covered streets. The lacy coverings for bazaars recall works by the Bay Area's Dottie Reid, and the clustered groupings of houses clinging tenaciously to hillsides remind one of nothing so much as the extraordinary villages of thumbnail-size buildings created out of miniscule handmade clay bricks by Charles Simonds and inserted into cracks and crevices of normal city/ghetto streets and, occasionally, in a museum or on a gallery wall.

The ambition of her own "psycho-architecture," as she calls it, is to make architecture once again an emblem of the deepest human desire, to make it an expressive performance, to restore to it that sense of compulsion which sweeps us away from ourselves to a wish to be ourselves more completely and deeply. It is the dream that all the arts have, the magic they mean to make.

Donald B. Kuspit, "Aycock's Dream Houses," *Art in America*, September 1980, p. 87.

In this growth of landscape-art into a slow transformation of the world into landscape, there is a long human development. The content of these pictures, resulting so unintentionally from observation and work, speaks to us of a future that has begun in our own time: tells us that man is no longer the social entity, moving with poise amongst his like, nor is he any longer one for whom evening and morning, for whom proximity and distance exist. It tells us, that he is placed amongst things like a thing, infinitely alone, and that all which is common to them both has withdrawn from things and men into the common depth, where the roots of all growth drink.

Rainer Maria Rilke, *Where Silence Reigns* (New York: New Directions, 1978), p. 5.

Simonds' house as body as vessel, with its pink, folded vaginal canyons and all of its earthy sexual clay overtones, are some of the most exquisitely erotic works of contemporary sculpture.

There is no space nor is there a need to list in this essay all of the artists included in this exhibition, nor do I necessarily believe that those mentioned are among the most important. I have tried to write only about works I have seen and know about from firsthand experience. There are many others known to me only by reputation or from photographs. For this reason I look forward to the exhibition with anticipation.

And all the spaces of our past moments of solitude, the spaces in which we have suffered from solitude, enjoyed, desired and compromised solitude, remain indelible within us, and precisely because the human being wants them to remain so. He knows instinctively that this space identified with his solitude is creative . . . even when it is forever expunged from the present.

Gaston Bachelard, *The Poetics of Space* (New York: Beacon Press, 1969).

NOTES

1. Gaston Bachelard, *The Poetics of Space* (Boston: Beacon Press, 1969), p. 6.

2. Martin Heidegger, *Poetry, Language and Thought* (New York: Harper & Row, 1971), p. 158.

3. Lucy Lippard, *Overlay, Contemporary Art and the Art of Prehistory* (New York: Pantheon Books, 1983), p. 8.

4. Martin Heidegger, *Poetry, Language and Thought* (New York: Harper & Row, 1971), p. 157.

5. Ibid., p. 157.

6. Gaston Bachelard, *The Poetics of Space* (Boston: Beacon Press, 1969), p. 33.

7. Louis Barragan in Emilio Ambasz, *The Architecture of Louis Barragan* (New York: The Museum of Modern Art), Introduction.

8. Martin Heidegger, *Poetry, Language and Thought* (New York: Harper & Row, 1971), p. 155.

9. Paul Goldberger, *Mexican Wins Architecture Prize, New York Times News Service* (The Washington Star, June 6, 1980).

10. Albert Elsen, *The Purposes of Art* (New York: Holt, Reinhardt and Winston, Inc., 1962), p. vii.

11. Lucy Lippard, *Overlay, Contemporary Art and the Art of Prehistory* (New York: Pantheon Books, 1983), p. 5.

12. Ibid., p. 4.

If art is made for its own sake, actually the sake of the artist, then the artist can determine subject matter and the manner of presentation. A painter can select the canvas size, the type of paint and, of course, the particular gestures and images that are of interest to the artist and not dictated by church, government or even an academy of artists. Working alone, the artist has the frame for symbolic protection to wall in his intent and secure his identity. *But,* so much for symbolic protection.

An American artist born in Cologne, West Germany, Hans Haacke has created a number of art projects that have made artists painfully aware that framing is in the eye of the beholder. Just as the artist is capable of framing, so can the artist be framed.[1] Haacke has shown very clearly that the artist's work can, and usually does, pick up meanings regardless of and far beyond the artist's intent. Like it or not, what is inside the artist's frame is colored by the wall on which it hangs. Unfortunately, museum buildings, bastions of culture, which should be sensitive to the plight of artists, are not safe havens. Haacke projects such as *MOMA-Poll*, 1970; *Solomon R. Guggenheim Museum Board of Trustees*, 1974; and *The Master Chocolate-Maker*, 1981, have illustrated that the smooth, white walls of the museum are not the neutral supports they are usually thought to be.

As artists have become increasingly aware of this situation, some have chosen to bring architecture into their work, to acknowledge the characteristics of architecture and, in some cases, to color the architecture with their art. Often this requires removing the symbolic frame and blurring the edges, and usually it has not been painters who have chosen this direction. A particular problem for painters is that most of their work is portable and, therefore, subject to the whims (intentional or otherwise)[2] of those who own or have temporary custody of the work of art.

In an attempt to gain more control over their own art—to build better frames—some painters, such as Mark Rothko, have accepted commissions for the permanent installation of their work. For the Rothko Chapel in Houston, he painted fourteen separate panels, which were installed to his specifications[3] around the octagonal interior. Most viewers see the paintings as a continuum: a single, three-dimensional painting. There are no frames on the panels; the frame is the building itself. Working with architect Philip Johnson,[4] the artist wanted to place a literal wall around his work. It was Rothko's intent to de-emphasize the building structure in order to create a place where visitors could experience the paintings without interference.

Siah Armajani deals with architecture in another way. He is thought of as a sculptor, but the objects he builds are not his art. It might be more accurate to call him a frame-maker. In a recent exhibition at the Baxter Art Gallery at the California Institute of Technology in Pasadena, the artist constructed *A Poetry Lounge*.[5] This was not a static tableau, rather the gallery was transformed to a functioning poetry lounge. I say "functioning" because that's what

BY MICHAEL H. SMITH

happened. The artist didn't make it happen, he made the place for it to happen. His work framed the activity.

Into the gallery the artist brought desks, shelves, tables, benches, a podium, books and even a coat rack. All of the objects were custom designed by Armajani, who made them in his studio in Minneapolis for the installation in California. For ease of assembly, many pieces were put together and held in place by hinges. This was, perhaps, a practical decision like his choice of standard, Sears paints, so touchups would be no problem. To me, though, the hinges emphasized that the installation was temporary and at some future time would be disassembled, packed up, and reassembled someplace else. Maybe others were not so aware of this because, as noted, Armajani's furniture and wall details were precisely designed for that particular place. Even so, the artist seemed to be suggesting that, like paintings, frames—even architectural frames—are portable.

Another artist, Richard Tuttle, has presented an entirely different view of framing. In 1977 he created 210 collage-drawings on spiral-bound drawing paper, either seventeen-by-fourteen inches or fourteen-by-eleven inches. Later, the artist conceived a way of showing these drawings in a series of installations at different exhibition spaces. Instead of displaying the entire body of work each time, Tuttle, on site, made a selection. Although each presentation carried the same title, "From 210 Collage-Drawings," each differed dependent on the choices he made.

What was unsettling to many who saw the exhibition was that the drawings were not framed. The artist tore the sheets from their binder and affixed them directly to the wall in a temporary and uncharacteristically (for museums) vulnerable fashion. Without traditional frames, the walls literally served as active support for the artwork.

But on another level, Tuttle brought into question what was supporting what. Most likely only those who saw more than one installation of "From 210 Collage-Drawings" would have been aware that, regardless of wall height, all the drawings in all the installations were attached to the walls with the midpoint of each sheet 64½ inches from the floor.

As curator of the initial presentation,[6] I thought this was a rather strange thing for the artist to determine beforehand. Within the three rooms that formed the gallery, wall heights vary, and there are some odd features that influence how artworks look in that space. I usually considered each room a separate visual problem. I wondered, too, about other places the works were to be presented. Surely the curators at those different places would have different ideas about "hanging" the art.

That, however, was Tuttle's point: what is being done to what? The constant is the artist's drawings; the variable is the architecture. In a delicate yet powerful way, Richard Tuttle turned things inside out and put a paper frame around the museums.

Tuttle, Armajani, the late Mark Rothko and Haacke, as well as many others working today, have demonstrated the power artists have to create their own place for presenting their art. By looking at, recognizing, sometimes accepting and sometimes altering the varied meanings architecture projects, artists are able to use this information as their own frame for building their art. Instead of being locked out, artists have moved right in and have begun to set up house.

Michael H. Smith
April 1983

PLATE 2 SIAH ARMAJANI, *A POETRY LOUNGE*, 1982
(DETAIL OF INSTALLATION, BAXTER ART GALLERY, CALIFORNIA INSTITUTE OF TECHNOLOGY, PASADENA, CA)
PHOTOGRAPHED BY GREY CRAWFORD

NOTES
1. Hans Haacke, *Framing and Being Framed* (New York: New York University Press, 1975).
2. Henri Matisse's drawing, "Le Bateau," was hung upside down by The Museum of Modern Art, New York, for forty-seven days. It is estimated 116,000 people passed through the gallery (Norris McWhirter, *Guinness Book of World Records* [New York: Bantam Books, 1978], pp. 199–200.
3. Mark Rothko died February 25, 1970. The Rothko Chapel was completed in January 1971.
4. Philip Johnson originally collaborated with Mark Rothko, but the building was completed by Howard Barnstone and Eugene Aubry.
5. Michael H. Smith, *Siah Armajani: A Poetry Lounge*, exhbition catalogue (Pasadena: Baxter Art Gallery, 1982).
6. Susan C. Larson, *Richard Tuttle: From 210 Collage-Drawings*, exhibition catalogue (Pasadena: Baxter Art Gallery, 1980).

LEGEND:

*Sans * denotes works in the gallery space.*
*   denotes works in the slide-sound presentation.
**   denotes work in the gallery space and in the slide-sound presentation.
Height precedes width precedes depth.

ARTISTS IN THE EXHIBITION

PLATE 3   *ADAMS' HOUSE,* 1977

24

STATEMENT

I see my two houses, the "Adams' House" of 1977 and "The Lost House" of 1979 as containers of my own most important personal memories. "Adams' House" was based on the construction and detailing of the house where I grew up. Dedicated to my parents who died shortly before this sculpture was built, "Adams' House" was the container of my childhood and gave me the chance to go home again.

"The Lost House" is a vision from a favorite novel, *Le Grand Meulnes*, by Alain Fournier. Set in France's Massif Central where I had spent an important year of my life in 1953, it is all about NOT being able to go home again.

Since then, my work has become more site oriented and site involved.

Alice Adams, 1983

SELECTED BIOGRAPHY
Born in New York, New York, 1930
Lives in New York, New York

Selected Honors
1981 Guggenheim Fellowship
1980 Short-term Fellow in the Humanities, Princeton University, NJ
1978 National Endowment for the Arts, Artist's Fellowship
1976 New York State Council on the Arts, Creative Artists Public Service Grant
1972 New York State Council on the Arts, Creative Artists Public Service Grant
1953 French Government Fellowship, Fulbright Travel Grant to Aubusson, France

Selected Solo Exhibitions
1983 Hammarskjold Plaza, New York, NY
1981 Hal Bromm Gallery, New York, NY
1980 Artemesia Gallery, Chicago, IL
     Public Art Fund, City Hall Park, New York, NY
1979 Hal Bromm Gallery, New York, NY
1975 55 Mercer Street Gallery, New York, NY
1974 55 Mercer Street Gallery, New York, NY
1973 55 Mercer Street Gallery, New York, NY
1971 55 Mercer Street Gallery, New York, NY
1964 Blumenfeld Gallery, New York, NY

Selected Site Works
1982 "From the Center," Belmont Park, Dayton, OH
1980 "The Globe," P.S. 1, The Institute for Art and Urban Resources, Queens, NY
     "Lost House," Neuberger Museum, State University of New York, College at Purchase, NY
     "The Globe," City Hall Park, New York, NY
     "Mound for Viewing Slope and Sky," Princeton University, NJ
1979 "Lost House," Wave Hill, Riverdale, NY
1977 "Levelling," Wilson College, Chambersburg, PA
     "Adams' House," Nassau County Museum of Fine Arts, Roslyn, NY
     "Three Structures on a Slope," Queensborough Community College, Bayside, NY
     "Shorings," ArtPark, Lewiston, NY
1974 "Greensboro Column," Weatherspoon Gallery, University of North Carolina, Greensboro, NC

Selected Group Exhibitions
1982 "Women Sculptors' Drawings," Hutchinson Gallery, New York, NY
1981 "The Image of the House in Contemporary Art," University of Houston, Lawndale Annex, TX (cat.)
     Heresies Art Auction, Grey Art Gallery, New York, NY
     "The Summer Show," Hal Bromm Gallery, New York, NY
1980 P.S. 1, The Institute for Art and Urban Resources, New York, NY
     "New York: 1980," Banco Gallery, Brescia, Italy
     "Sitesights," Pratt Institute, Brooklyn, NY
     "The National Invitational Sculpture Show," Maryland College Institute of Art, Baltimore, MD
     "The Summer Show," Hal Bromm Gallery, New York, NY
     "Architectural Sculpture," Los Angeles Institute of Contemporary Art, CA (cat.)
     "Drawings," Hal Bromm Gallery, New York. NY
1979 "Drawings," Hal Bromm Gallery, New York, NY
     "The Artists' View," Wave Hill, Riverdale, NY (cat.)
     "New Editions: Adams, Chamberlain, Hall, Highstein," Hal Bromm Gallery, New York, NY
1978 "Outdoor Sculpture and Works Inside," Queensborough Community College, Bayside, NY
     "Alice Adams/Rosemarie Castoro," Rush Rhees Gallery, University of Rochester, NY
     "Sculpture," P.S. 1, The Institute for Art and Urban Resources, Queens, NY
     "Sculpture," Hal Bromm Gallery, New York, NY
     Artist-in-Residence, ArtPark, Lewiston, NY
     "Architectural Analogues," Whitney Museum Downtown Branch, New York, NY (cat.)
     "Dwellings," Institute of Contemporary Art, University of Pennsylvania, Philadelphia, PA (circulated: Neuberger Museum, State University of New York, College at Purchase, NY) (cat.)
1977 "Wood," Nassau County Museum of Fine Arts, Roslyn, NY
1975 "Spare," East Hall Gallery, Port Washington, NY
     Herbert Lehman College Gallery, New York, NY
1974 "New York Eleven," C.W. Post Center Art Gallery, Greenvale, NY
     "Painting and Sculpture Today," Indianapolis Museum of Art, IN
1973 "The Whitney Biennial Exhibition of Painting and Sculpture," Whitney Museum of American Art, New York, NY
     "Sculpture 3," World Trade Center, New York, NY
1972 "GEDOK American Women Artist Show," Kunsthaus, Hamburg, West Germany
     "13 Women," 117 Prince Street, New York, NY
1971 "Annual Exhibition of Contemporary American Sculpture," Whitney Museum of American Art, New York, NY
     "Penthouse Gallery," The Museum of Modern Art, New York, NY
1966 "Miniature Tapestries," Museum of Contemporary Crafts, New York, NY
1963 "Woven Forms," Museum of Contemporary Crafts, New York, NY
1961 "American Tapestries," Victoria and Albert Museum, London, England
1958 "Fulbright Designers," Museum of Contemporary Crafts, New York, NY

WORKS IN THE EXHIBITION

"Three Structures on a Slope," 1978*
50' x 60,' wood
Site: Queensborough Community College, Bayside, NY

"Adams' House," 1977 (plate 3)*
28' x 12' x 10,' wood
Site: Nassau County Museum of Fine Arts, Roslyn, NY
Photographed by Bill Gordy

ALICE ADAMS

PLATE 4   *DICTIONARY FOR BUILDING: ATTIC WINDOW–GROUND FLOOR WINDOW, 1979–81*
PLATE 5   *DICTIONARY FOR BUILDING: ATTIC DOOR, 1979–81*

26

STATEMENT

To build open, available, useful, low, near, common public gathering places. Not as a thing between four walls in a geometric spatial sense but as a tool which directs us into a place for living.

Siah Armajani, 1983

SELECTED BIOGRAPHY

Born in Tehran, Iran, 1939
Lives in St. Paul, Minnesota

Selected Solo Exhibitions

1983 Max Protetch Gallery, New York, NY
1982 Baxter Art Gallery, California Institute of Technology, Pasadena, CA (cat.)
Grand Rapids Art Museum, MI
Samuel S. Fleisher Art Memorial, Philadelphia, PA
1981 Max Protetch Gallery, New York, NY
The Hudson River Museum, Yonkers, NY (cat.)
1980 Joslyn Art Museum, Omaha, NB (cat.)
Contemporary Arts Center, Cincinnati, OH
1979 Ohio State University, Columbus, OH
Max Protetch Gallery, New York, NY (circulated: Landmark Center, St. Paul, MN)
University of Illinois at Chicago Circle, IL
Kansas City Art Institute, MO
The New Gallery of Contemporary Art, Cleveland, OH
1978 Philadelphia College of Art, PA (circulated: Alternative Spaces Residency Program, Dayton, OH) (cat.)
Cranbrook Academy of Art, Bloomfield Hills, MI

Selected Permanent Site Works

1983 "NOAA Bridge," Seattle, WA
1982 "The Louis I. Kahn Lecture Room," Samuel S. Fleisher Art Memorial, Philadelphia, PA
1980 "Reading Garden No. 1," Roanoke College, VA

Selected Video

1976 "Skylight at Monticello," University Art Museum, University of California, Berkeley, CA

Selected Group Exhibitions

1983 "Five Sculptors," Seattle Art Museum Pavilion, Seattle, WA
"Directions 1983," Hirshhorn Museum and Sculpture Garden, Smithsonian Institution, Washington, D.C.
"Habitats," The Clocktower, New York, NY
"Connections: Bridges/Ladders/Ramps/Staircases/Tunnels," Institute of Contemporary Art, University of Pennsylvania, Philadelphia, PA
"Sculpture as Architecture," Thomas Segal Gallery, Boston, MA
1982 "Form and Function: Proposals for Public Art for Philadelphia," Pennsylvania Academy of the Fine Arts, Philadelphia, PA
"Seventy-fourth American Exhibition," The Art Institute of Chicago, IL
"Dokumenta 7," Kassel, West Germany
"Post Minimalism," Aldrich Museum of Contemporary Art, Ridgefield, CT
1981 "The Whitney Biennial Exhibition of Painting and Sculpture," Whitney Museum of American Art, New York, NY (cat.)
"Architecture by Artists," Rosa Esman Gallery, New York, NY
"Artists' Gardens and Parks," Hayden Gallery, Massachusetts Institute of Technology, Cambridge, MA (circulated: Museum of Contemporary Art, Chicago, IL)
"The Image of the House in Contemporary Art," University of Houston, Lawndale Annex, TX (cat.)
"Metaphor: New Projects by Contemporary Sculptors," Hirshhorn Museum and Sculpture Garden, Smithsonian Institution, Washington, D.C. (cat.)
1980 "ArtPark '80," ArtPark, Lewiston, NY (cat.)
XIII Winter Olympic Games, Lake Placid, NY (cat.)
"Drawings/Sculptures," Institute of Contemporary Art, Boston, MA
"Drawings: The Pluralist Decade," 39th Venice Biennale, United States Pavilion, Italy (circulated: Institute of Contemporary Art, University of Pennsylvania, Philadelphia, PA; Museum of Contemporary Art, Chicago, IL) (cat.)

"Architectural Sculpture," Los Angeles Institute of Contemporary Art, CA (cat.)
1979 "Art and Architecture, Space and Structure," Protetch-McIntosh Gallery, Washington, D.C.
"The Artists' View," Wave Hill, Riverdale, NY (cat.)
"Mind, Child Architecture," The Newark Museum, NJ
1978 "Indoor-Outdoor," P.S. 1, The Institute for Art and Urban Resources, Long Island City, NY
"Inaugural Exhibition," Max Protetch Gallery, New York, NY
"Young American Artists," Exxon National Exhibition, The Solomon R. Guggenheim Museum, New York, NY (cat.)
"Architectural Analogues," Whitney Museum Downtown Branch, New York, NY (cat.)
"Dwellings," Institute of Contemporary Art, University of Pennsylvania, Philadelphia, PA (circulated: Neuberger Museum, State University of New York, College at Purchase, NY) (cat.)
1977 "Scale and Environment, 10 Sculptors," Walker Art Center, Minneapolis, MN (cat.)
1977- "16 Projects/4 Artists: Siah Armajani, Larry Bell, Lloyd Hamrol,
76   Pat Steir," Court House Square, Dayton, OH (circulated: Moore College of Art, Philadelphia, PA; University of Kentucky, Lexington, KY) (cat.)
1976 "Virtual Reality," Carpenter Center for the Visual Arts, Harvard University, Cambridge, MA
California State University, Long Beach, CA
1975 "Sculpture for a New Era," Federal Center, Chicago, IL (cat.)
1974 "Discussions: Works/Words," P.S. 1, The Institute for Art and Urban Resources, The Clocktower, New York, NY
1972 "Dokumenta 5," Kassel, West Germany
"Operation Vesuvius," Henry Gallery, University of Washington, Seattle, WA (circulated: Galleria d'Arte il Centro, Naples, Italy)
"The Boardwalk Show," Convention Hall, Atlantic City, NJ
"Drawings: 10 Minnesota Artists," Walker Art Center, Minneapolis, MN
1970 "Art in the Mind," Allen Memorial Art Museum, Oberlin College, OH (cat.)
"Information," The Museum of Modern Art, New York, NY (cat.)
"9 Artists/9 Spaces," Minnesota State Arts Council, MN (cat.)
"Architectural Entities," University of Montana, Missoula, MT
1969 "Art by Telephone," Museum of Contemporary Art, Chicago, IL
"Painting and Sculpture Today, '69," Indianapolis Museum of Art, IN (cat.)
"Towers," Museum of Contemporary Art, Chicago, IL (circulated: Museum of Art, Finch College, New York, NY)

WORKS IN THE EXHIBITION

"Dictionary for Building: Attic Window—Ground Floor Window," 1979–81 (plate 4)
96" × 28½" × 14," painted wood, aluminum and plexiglass
Lent by Max Protetch Gallery, New York, NY
Photographed by James Casebere

"Dictionary for Building: Attic Door," 1979–81 (plate 5)
92" × 27½" × 26½," redwood, aluminum and plexiglass
Lent by Max Protetch Gallery, New York, NY
Photographed by James Casebere

"Newstand," 1980*
11' × 38' × 98,' wood, plexiglass and paint
Site: Contemporary Arts Center, Cincinnati, OH

SIAH ARMAJANI

PLATE 6   *EXPLANATION, AN, OF SPRING AND THE WEIGHT OF AIR*, 1979

28

STATEMENT

In my earlier, more architectural sculpture, I had been involved with the exploration of how one orients oneself in the world through the six dimensions of space: up, down, left, right, backwards and forwards. Having reached a level of understanding and familiarity of the mental states such as claustrophobia and acrophilia in my earlier mazes, underground tunnels and towering complexes, I moved to thinking about less known and concrete mental spaces where one finds oneself in a disorienting, perhaps weightless setting, where up and down and right and left give less information and fewer answers. I thought about the experience of being on a roller coaster, of being freed from gravity. It seemed to me that the disjunction, the uncertainty, the ambiguity that I experienced could be articulated. In the past, using the conventional vocabulary or sign system of architecture—doors, walls, roofs, ladders, floors, shafts, wells—as a set of directions for a performance (as a structure for an event), I tried to create a vocabulary of disjunction. My more recent work has left the realm of architecture for a more mechanical, industrial vocabulary, nevertheless I continue to think about the sensations felt by atomic particles being shattered by atom smasher, by ghosts being manufactured, by angels writing in the sky, by bits of information moving through the structure of the mind as it thinks. I try to envision and invent worlds in which the experiences encountered are more fantastic, wondrous and awesome than those we confront day to day, where causality and logic play a minor role and where what seems to be impossible feats can perhaps be accomplished.

Alice Aycock, 1983

SELECTED BIOGRAPHY

Born in Harrisburg, Pennsylvania, 1946
Lives in New York, New York

Selected Solo Exhibitions

1983   "The Nets Of Solomon, Phase II," Museum of Contemporary Art, Chicago, IL
"The Thousand and One Nights In The Mansion Of Bliss," Protetch-McNeil Gallery, New York, NY
"One Thousand and One Nights In The Mansion of Bliss Part II, The Fortress of Utopia," Wurttembergischer Kunstverein Stuttgart, West Germany
1982   "A Theory For Universal Causality (Time/Creation Machines)," Lawrence Oliver Gallery, Philadelphia, PA
"The Miraculating Machine In The Garden (Tower Of The Winds)," Douglass College, New Brunswick, NJ
1982, John Weber Gallery, New York, NY
81,78
1981   "The Savage Sparkler," State University of Plattsburgh, NY
1980   "The Game Of Fliers," Washington Public Arts, Washington, D.C.
"Collected Ghost Stories From The Workhouse," University of South Florida, Tampa, FL
1979   "Explanation, An, Of Spring and the Weight of Air," Contemporary Arts Center, Cincinnati, OH
"How To Catch and Manufacture Ghosts," and "The Machine That Makes The World," John Weber Gallery, New York, NY
1978   "A Precarious Method for Attacking an Enemy Fortress . . .," Portland Center for Visual Arts, OR
"On The Eve Of The Industrial Revolution, A City Engaged In The Production Of False Miracles," Cranbrook Academy of Art, Bloomfield Hills, MI
1977   "The World Is So Full of a Number of Things," 112 Greene Street Gallery, New York, NY
"Studies For A Town," Project Room, The Museum of Modern Art, New York, NY
1976   "Circular Building With Narrow Ledges For Walking," Fry Farm, Silver Springs, PA
1973   "Low Building With Dirt Roof (For Mary)," Gibney Farm, New Kingston, PA
1972   Nova Scotia College of Art and Design, Halifax, Nova Scotia, Canada

Selected Group Exhibitions

1983   "The 1983 Sculpture Invitational," Oscarsson Hood Gallery, New York, NY
"1984—A Preview," Ronald Feldman Fine Arts Gallery, New York, NY
"Connections," Institute of Contemporary Art, University of Pennsylvania, Philadelphia, PA
"Recent Acquisitions: Works On Paper," The Solomon R. Guggenheim Museum, New York, NY
"International Water Sculpture Competition, Pre-finalists Exhibition," 1984 Louisiana World Exposition, New Orleans, LA
"Het Idee Van De Stad," Kunst Actualiteiten Arnhem, The Netherlands (major installation)
"Biennale 17," Middelheim, Antwerpen, Belgium (major installation)
"Codici e Marchingegni 1482/1983," Museo Leonardian, Vinci, Italy
"Knot and Spiral Show," Suellen Haber Gallery, New York, NY
1982   "Venice Biennale," Italy
Fattoria de Celle, Pistoria, Italy (major installation)
1981   "Machineworks: Alice Aycock, Vito Acconci, Dennis Oppenheim," Institute of Contemporary Art, University of Pennsylvania, Philadelphia, PA (major installation)
"Myth & Ritual," Kunsthaus, Zurich, Switzerland (major installation)
"Collaboration: Artists and Architects," New York Historical Society, New York, NY
"The Whitney Biennial Exhibition of Painting and Sculpture," Whitney Museum of American Art, New York, NY (cat.)
"The Soft Land," Ortona Palazzo Farnese, Ortona, Italy (major installation)
"Natur-Skulptur," Wurttembergischer Kunstverein, Stuttgart, West Germany
"The Image of the House in Contemporary Art," University of Houston, Lawndale Annex, TX (cat.)
"Metaphor, New Projects by Contemporary Sculptors," Hirshhorn Museum and Sculpture Garden, Smithsonian Institution, Washington, D.C. (major installation)
1980   "Architectural References," Vancouver Art Gallery, British Columbia, Canada (cat.)

WORKS IN THE EXHIBITION

"Explanation, An, Of Spring and the Weight of Air," 1979 (plate 6)*
18' × 18' × 36,' wood
Site: Contemporary Arts Center, Cincinnati, OH
Photographed by Alice Aycock

"The Tread Mill" (from "On The Eve Of The Industrial Revolution, A City Engaged In The Production Of False Miracles"), 1978*
18' × 10' × 15,' wood
Site: Cranbrook Academy of Art, Bloomfield Hills, CA

"An Explanation For The Rainbow" (from "On The Eve Of The Industrial Revolution, A City Engaged In The Production of False Miracles"), 1978*
15' × 12' × 15,' wood
Site: Cranbrook Academy of Art, Bloomfield Hills, MI

ALICE AYCOCK

PLATE 7   *ZOBOP CAYE,* 1983

30

STATEMENT

I do not preconceive my images. I begin with a horizontal surface (the ground); I build a structure. If it is a house or another "combination," the unconscious decisions are there to be received as communications. From combined fragments I try to construct a whole, both in a physical and psychological sense. Materials and final form mean precisely the same to me as any more commonly used medium.

I am not interested in depicting objective reality, but believe in the unknown, the mysterious, the enigmatic as the logical sources of my work. Sheen, finish, newness are questionable given time, history and memory.

Don Baum, 1983

SELECTED BIOGRAPHY

Born in Escanaba, Michigan, 1922
Lives in Chicago, Illinois

Selected Honors

1977   Award for Outstanding Contribution in the Arts, Cliff Dweller's Club, Chicago, IL
1973   American Commissioner of the United States entry in Sao Paulo Bienal, Brazil

Selected Solo Exhibitions

1982   "Don Baum," Betsy Rosenfield Gallery, Inc., Chicago, IL
1981   "Don Baum: A Review of Works from 1947-1981," Hyde Park Art Center, Chicago, IL
1980   "Don Baum," Betsy Rosenfield Gallery, Inc., Chicago, IL
1965   "Don Baum: Chicago Objects," The Bridge Gallery, New York, NY
       "Don Baum Constructions," The John L. Hunt Gallery, Chicago, IL
1963   "Don Baum Constructions," The John L. Hunt Gallery, Chicago, IL
1961   "Don Baum: Paintings–Drawings–Collages–Constructions," Hyde Park Art Center, Chicago, IL

Selected Group Exhibitions

1983   "Chicago Artists: Continuity and Change," Printers Row Exhibition Space, Chicago, IL
       "Shelter Show," Evanston Art Center, IL
1983- "Collage and Assemblage," Mississippi Museum of Art,
81   Jackson, MS
1982   "Poetic Objects," Washington Project for the Arts, Washington, D.C.
       "Hot Chicago," Douglas Drake Gallery, Kansas City, KS
       "Chicago Imagists," Kansas City Art Institute, MO
       "62nd Annual Artists Members Exhibition," The Arts Club of Chicago, IL
1981   "City Sculpture," The Cultural Center of the Chicago Public Library, IL
       "Collector's Choice," St. Louis Museum of Art, MO
       "The Image of the House in Contemporary Art," University of Houston, Lawndale Annex, TX (cat.)
1980   "Paperworks and Sculpture: 60th Annual Exhibition by the Professional Members," The Arts Club, Chicago, IL
       "Selections from the Collection of Arthur Paul and the Paintings and Drawings of Arthur Paul," Columbia Gallery of Columbia College, Chicago, IL
       "Some Recent Art from Chicago," William Hayes Ackland Memorial Art Center, University of North Carolina, Chapel Hill, NC
       "Collage 1," Evanston Art Center, IL
       "100 Artists, 100 Years: Alumni of the School of the Art Institute of Chicago," Centennial Exhibition, The Art Institute of Chicago, IL
1979   "31st Illinois Invitational," Illinois State Museum, Springfield, IL
1976   "Dolls! Dolls! Dolls!," Gallery 2269, Chicago, IL
       "Hyde Park Art Center Retrospective Exhibition: Historic Panorama Abra Cadabra," Chicago, IL
1975   "Dolls and Other Effigies," John Michael Kohler Arts Center, Sheboygan, WI
1973   "Seventy-fourth Exhibition by Artists of Chicago and Vicinity," The Art Institute of Chicago, IL
1972   "Chicago Imagist Art," Museum of Contemporary Art, Chicago, IL (circulated: The New York Cultural Center, New York, NY)
       "Point/Counterpoint: Don Baum and June Leaf," Galerie le chat Bernard, Chicago, IL
       "Santi-Cloth," Hyde Park Art Center, Chicago, IL
1971   "Astrology is the Clock of Destiny," Hyde Park Art Center, Chicago, IL
       "Art After Art," The Renaissance Society at the University of Chicago, IL
1970   "Famous Artists from Chicago," Madison Art Center, WI

PLATE 8   *PITTSLEY'S PAPERS*, 1980

WORKS IN THE EXHIBITION

"Zobop Caye," 1983 (plate 7)
16½" × 17¼" × 11¼," wood
Lent by Betsy Rosenfield Gallery, Inc., Chicago, IL
Photographed by Tom Van Eynde

"Blues House," 1982*
17" × 18½" × 17½," wood

"Hunting Camp," 1981*
12" × 18" × 15," wood and feathers

"House of Music," 1981*
16½" × 24" × 18," wood

"Pittsley's Papers," 1980 (plate 8)
11" × 7" × 14," wood, tarpaper and paper
Lent by Betty Asher
Photographed by Mark Schwartz

DON BAUM

PLATE 9   *PRISONER OF LOVE*, 1967

STATEMENT

I want to make both the scale of the viewer to the works and the scale of the sculptures to the enclosing room strongly felt. It is important that they be seen in an interior space where they can be seen as buildings, inside of buildings, inside of a building.

I did not want them to be objects, or to be architecture, but to exist as a category by themselves.

In an allegorical sense they represent the unity of male and female elements, of the past and present. In the end each work has the specific quality of a portrait.

In making these sculptures with their maze-like-crystal-like, forest-like qualities, I wanted to create not just a work, but a place.

From Tony Berlant in *The Image of the House in Contemporary Art* (University of Houston, Lawndale Annex, 1982).

SELECTED BIOGRAPHY

Born in New York, New York, 1941
Lives in Santa Monica, California, and New York, New York

Selected Honors
1964   New Talent Purchase Award, Contemporary Arts Council, Los Angeles County Museum of Art, CA
1962   Ford Foundation Purchase Award, The Museum of Fine Arts, Houston, TX

Selected Solo Exhibitions
1983   John Berggruen Gallery, San Francisco, CA
1982   Houston Museum of Contemporary Art, TX
       "Tony Berlant: New Works," Xavier-Fourcade, Inc., New York, NY
       L.A. Louver, Venice, CA
1981   "Tony Berlant Recent Work," Conejo Valley Art Museum, Thousand Oaks, CA
1979   "Sculptural Perspectives," Art Museum, University of California, Santa Barbara, CA
       James Corcoran Gallery, Los Angeles, CA
1978   "Tony Berlant," Newport Harbor Art Museum, Newport Beach, CA
       "Tony Berlant Constructions & Collages," Texas Gallery, Houston, TX
1977   James Corcoran Gallery, Los Angeles, CA
1976   "Cubes and Quilts," Texas Gallery, Houston, TX
1975   "James Corcoran Gallery, Los Angeles, CA
1974   Phyllis Kind Gallery, Chicago, IL
1973   "Tony Berlant: The Marriage of New York and Athens," Whitney Museum of American Art, New York, NY (circulated)
1971   Mizuno Gallery, Los Angeles, CA
       Wichita Art Museum, KS
1967, David Stuart Gallery, Los Angeles, CA
65
1964   Hansen Gallery, San Francisco, CA
1963   David Stuart Gallery, Los Angeles, CA

Selected Group Exhibitions
1983   "Young Talent Awards: 1963-1983," Los Angeles County Museum of Art, CA (cat.)
1981   "The Image of the House in Contemporary Art," University of Houston, Lawndale Annex, TX (cat.)
       "California: A Sense of Individualism," L.A. Louver, Venice, CA
       "Artists' Quilts," La Jolla Museum of Contemporary Art, La Jolla, CA
1980   Xavier Fourcade, Inc., New York, NY
       "Architectural Sculpture," Los Angeles Institute of Contemporary Art (Downtown), CA (cat.)
1979   "Sculptural Perspectives: An Exhibition of Small Sculpture of the '70s," University of California, Santa Barbara, CA
1978   "Dwellings," Institute of Contemporary Art, University of Pennsylvania, Philadelphia, PA (circulated: Neuberger Museum, State University of New York, College at Purchase, NY) (cat.)

1977   "A Question of Scale," School of Visual Arts, New York, NY
       "Art from Los Angeles," The Museum of Modern Art, New York, NY
1974   "Painting and Sculpture Today," Indianapolis Museum of Art, IN
1973   "The Whitney Biennial Exhibition of Painting and Sculpture," Whitney Museum of American Art, New York, NY
       "The Emerging Real: Painting and Sculpture 1973," Storm King Art Center, Mountainville, NY
1972   "Working in California," Albright-Knox Art Gallery, Buffalo, NY
       "Seventieth American Exhibition," The Art Institute of Chicago, IL
       "12 Statements Beyond the Sixties," The Detroit Institute of Arts, MI
1971   "New Works by Los Angeles Artists," Los Angeles County Museum of Art, CA
1970   "Annual Exhibition of Contemporary American Sculpture," Whitney Museum of American Art, New York, NY
       "The West Coast Now," Joslyn Art Museum, Omaha, NB
1969   "Contemporary American Sculpture: Selection 2," Whitney Museum of American Art, New York, NY (circulated)
1968   "Annual Exhibition of Contemporary American Sculpture," Whitney Museum of American Art, New York, NY
1967   "American Sculpture of the Sixties," Los Angeles County Museum of Art, CA (circulated: Philadelphia Museum of Art, PA)

PLATE 10   *MISS CONSTANCE'S HOUSE*, 1965

WORKS IN THE EXHIBITION

Installation at Whitney Museum of American Art, 1973*

"The Last Temple," 1968
164" × 72" × 72," Zolatone paint over fiberglass over plywood

"The Forest," 1967
183" × 96" × 96," Zolatone paint over fiberglass over plywood

"The Marriage of New York and Athens," 1966
124" × 72" × 72," stainless steel over plywood

"Adam and Eve," 1968–79*
14" × 10" × 14¾," tin, nails, enamels, seashell and resin

"Prisoner of Love," 1967 (plate 9)
14⅝" × 10" × 14," found metal collage with brads over plywood; polyester resin; plaster figure and metal cage with enamel
Lent by the artist
Photographed by Susan Einstein

"Miss Constance's House," 1965 (plate 10)
53" × 21½" × 22¾," enameled steel on plywood with brads and polyester resin
Lent by Frank and Berta Gehry
Photographed by Mark Schwartz

TONY BERLANT

33

PLATE 11   *MOUNTAIN HOME*, 1983

34

STATEMENT

The use of the house in my work came about after actually acquiring the house where we live. It occurred to me that it had become an extension of my identity, not only in how I identified with it but also how it would be identified with me. The fact that there is an interior and an exterior and the idea of a parallel between the conscious and the unconscious as an architectural form provides endless possibilities. A house might acquire wisdom and the space within become more vast than the exterior would indicate.

John Buck, 1983

SELECTED BIOGRAPHY

Born in Ames, Iowa, 1946
Lives in Bozeman, Montana

Selected Honors

1980 National Endowment for the Arts, Artist's Fellowship
1972 Teaching Fellowship, Gloucester College of Art and Design, Cheltenham, England
1971 Scholarship, Skowhegan School of Sculpture and Painting
1970 Federal Fellowship Education Allowance Fund
Mary Lou Osborne, University of California, Davis, CA
n.d. Purchase Award, Second Annual Shasta College Invitational Art Exhibit, Redding, CA
n.d. Purchase Award, University of California, Davis, CA

Selected Solo Exhibitions

1983 Fuller Goldeen Gallery, San Francisco, CA
1983- "A Month of Sundays," Mandeville Art Gallery, University of
82 California, San Diego, CA (circulated: California State University, Fullerton, CA; Madison Art Center, WI; New Mexico State University, Las Cruces, NM; Concord Gallery, New York, NY)
1981, Hansen Fuller Goldeen Gallery, San Francisco, CA
79
1981 Morgan Gallery, Shawnee Mission, KS
1975 University of Kentucky, Lexington, KY
1974 Mira Costa College, Carlsbad, CA

Selected Group Exhibitions

1984- "Forgotton Dimension—A Survey of Small Sculpture in California
82 Now," Fresno Art Center, CA (circulated by Association of Art Museums) (cat.)
1983 "Corcoran Biennial," Corcoran Gallery of Art, Washington, D.C.
1982 "Painted Sculpture," Municipal Art Gallery, Barnsdall Park, Los Angeles, CA
"It Figures," Transamerica Corporation, San Francisco, CA
"Sculpture at U.C. Davis—Past and Present," University of California, Davis, CA
"The West as Art: Changing Perceptions of Western Art in California Collections," Palm Springs Desert Museum, CA (cat.)
1981 "The Figure: A Celebration," University of North Dakota Art Galleries, Grand Forks, ND (circulated: Art Museum of South Texas, Corpus Christi, TX)
1980 "Two-Man Show," Zolla Lieberman Gallery, Chicago, IL
Fendrick Gallery, Washington, D.C.
Alaska Center for the Visual Arts, Anchorage, AK
Triton Museum, Santa Clara, CA
Yellowstone Art Center, Billings, MT
"Painting and Sculpture Today," Indianapolis Museum of Art, IN
"The Peaceable Kingdom," Hansen Fuller Goldeen Gallery, San Francisco, CA
"Visions and Figurations," California State University, Fullerton, CA (cat.)
1980- "Western States Biennial," The Denver Art Museum, CO (circu-
79 lated: San Francisco Museum of Modern Art, CA; National Gallery of Art, Washington, D.C.; University of Hawaii, Honolulu, HI)
1979 Santa Clara Museum, CA
"Two-Man Show," Allan Frumkin Gallery, Chicago, IL
1978 "Invitational Group Show, Wood Sculpture," University of California, Davis, CA
1977 "Sculpture Exhibition," Central Washington State College, Ellens-

burg, WA
"Faculty Exhibition," Montana State University, Bozeman, MT
"Drawing Exhibition," Central Washington State College, Ellensburg, WA
University of California, Davis, CA
"Drawing Invitational," University of Montana, Missoula, MT
"Introductions Exhibition," Hansen Fuller Goldeen Gallery, San Francisco, CA
"San Francisco Art Institute Annual," invitational ceramics exhibition, CA
Hockaday Center for the Arts, Kalispell, MT
1975 Invitational Group Show, Morningside College, Sioux City, IA
1974 "Two-Man Faculty Exhibit," Humboldt State University, Arcata, CA
"Sculpture and Drawing Show," University of Nevada, Las Vegas, NV
"Clay Magic," Stephens College, Columbia, MO
"Faculty Exhibit," Humboldt State University, Arcata, CA
1973 University of Colorado, Boulder, CO
"Here We Go Gathering Nuts in May," The Candy Store, Folsom, CA
"Vacaville Crossing," Artist's Contemporary Sacramento Gallery, CA
1972 The Museum of Modern Art, Lending Gallery, New York, NY
"M.F.A. Show," University of California, Davis, CA
Artist's Contemporary Gallery, Sacramento, CA
"Ceramics," University of California, San Diego, CA
"Bay Area Underground," University Art Museum, Berkeley, CA
"Eight from Davis: Ceramic Sculpture," Wenger Gallery, San Francisco, CA
San Francisco Art Institute, CA
"Group Ceramic Show," San Francisco State College, CA
"Honig-Cooper and Harrington Art Awards Invitational," San Francisco, CA
1971 "Obscure Artists of Davis," University of California, Davis, CA
"A Group Show," University of Nevada, Reno, NV
"Second Annual Shasta College Invitational Art Exhibit," Redding, CA
"Doing Stuff with Feathers, Etc., Etc.," The Art Center of the World Gallery, Davis, CA
"Fifth Annual Juried Art Exhibition," Memorial Union Art Gallery, Davis, CA
1970 "Twenty-Four Hour Show," University of California, Davis, CA

WORK IN THE EXHIBITION

"Mountain Home," 1983 (plate 11)*
10' × 7,' painted wood and canvas
Photographed by M. Lee Fatherree

JOHN BUCK

PLATE 12   *HOUSE #1*, 1965

36

STATEMENT

Alone in Los Angeles, Celmins went through several years of introspection, recalling the war years of her childhood in Germany and the disastrous aftermath of the war. She recalled, "I had been collecting clippings. I would roam around Los Angeles. I didn't know anybody and I got little war books because it was kind of nostalgic." In 1965 these images appeared on the walls and roofs of two small-scale wooden houses, one which was adapted from a house on the Venice Circle and another which was a replica of a saltbox-style farmhouse of Indiana. . . .

In each of these house constructions, Celmins willfully and dramatically shifts scale, perspective, context. Her projected clouds and walls-as-windows recall the brilliant conceptual manipulations of Magritte while the specificity of her imagery, the autobiographical nature of it, adds the authentic accent of her own emotional involvement.

From Susan C. Larsen in *Vija Celmins: A Survey Exhibition,* (Fellows of Contemporary Art, Los Angeles, 1979), pp. 22–23.

SELECTED BIOGRAPHY
Born in Riga, Latvia, 1939
Lives in New York, New York

Selected Honors
1980   Guggenheim Fellowship
1976   National Endowment for the Arts, Artist's Fellowship
1971   National Endowment for the Arts, Artist's Fellowship
1968   Cassandra Foundation Award
1961   Yale University Summer Session Fellowship

Selected Solo Exhibitions
1983   David McKee Gallery, New York, NY
1980   "A Survey Exhibition," Newport Harbor Art Museum, Newport Beach, CA (circulated: Arts Club of Chicago, IL; The Hudson River Museum, Yonkers, NY; Corcoran Gallery of Art, Washington, D.C.) (cat.)
1978   Security Pacific National Bank, Los Angeles, CA
1975   Felicity Samuel Gallery, London, England
        Broxton Gallery, Los Angeles, CA
1973   Whitney Museum of American Art, New York, NY
1973, Mizuno Gallery, Los Angeles, CA
69
1966   David Stuart Galleries, Los Angeles, CA
1965   Dickson Art Center, University of California, Los Angeles, CA

Selected Group Exhibitions
1983- "Drawings by Painters," Long Beach Museum of Art, CA (circu-
82   lated: The Oakland Museum, CA)
1982   "Great Big Drawings, Contemporary Works on Paper," Hayden Gallery, Massachusetts Institute of Technology, Cambridge, MA
1981   "American Realism," Philadelphia Museum of Art, PA
        "The Image of the House in Contemporary Art," University of Houston, Lawndale Annex, TX (cat.)
        "California: The State of Landscape, 1872–1981," Newport Harbor Art Museum, Newport Beach, CA (cat.)
1979   "The Decade in Review: Selection of the 1970s," Whitney Museum of American Art, New York, NY
1977   "American Artists: A New Decade," The Detroit Institute of Arts, MI (circulated: Fort Worth Art Museum, TX; Grand Rapids Art Museum, MI)
        "Painting and Sculpture in California: The Modern Era," San Francisco Museum of Modern Art, CA (circulated: National Collection of Fine Arts, Smithsonian Institution, Washington, D.C.)
        "30 Years of American Printmaking," The Brooklyn Museum, NY
        "The Whitney Biennial Exhibition of Painting and Sculpture," Whitney Museum of American Art, New York, NY

1976   "America 1976," Corcoran Gallery of Art, Washington, D.C. (circulated: Wadsworth Atheneum, Hartford, CT; Fogg Art Museum, Cambridge, MA; The Minneapolis Institute of Arts, MN; Milwaukee Art Center, WI; Fort Worth Art Museum, TX; San Francisco Museum of Modern Art, CA; The High Museum of Art, Atlanta, GA; The Brooklyn Museum, NY)
1975   "A Drawing Show," Newport Harbor Art Museum, Newport Beach, CA
        "Recent Drawings," Huntsville Museum of Art, AL (circulated: Princeton University, NJ; Cummer Gallery of Art, Jacksonville, FL; State University of New York, Stony Brook, NY)
1974   "Seventy-first American Exhibition," The Art Institute of Chicago, IL
1973   "Ten Years of Contemporary Art Council Acquisitions," Los Angeles County Museum of Art, CA
        "American Drawings," Whitney Museum of American Art, New York, NY
1972   "California Prints," The Museum of Modern Art, New York, NY
        "A Survey of West Coast Art from the Permanent Collection and Loan Collections," Pasadena Art Museum, CA
        "L.A.," San Francisco Art Institute, CA
        "Eighteenth National Print Exhibition," The Brooklyn Museum, NY (circulated: California Palace of the Legion of Honor, San Francisco, CA)
1971   "Continuing Surrealism," La Jolla Museum of Contemporary Art, CA
        "24 Young Los Angeles Artists," Los Angeles County Museum of Art, CA
1970   "Annual Exhibition of Contemporary American Sculpture," Whitney Museum of American Art, New York, NY
1969   "Contemporary American Drawings," Fort Worth Art Museum, TX

WORKS IN THE EXHIBITION

"House #1," 1965 (plate 12)**
7¼" × 10½" × 9½," oil on wood, metal, fur and plastic
Lent by The Edward R. Broida Trust
Photographed by Frank J. Thomas

"House #2," 1965*
12" × 9¾" × 7," oil on wood and cardboard

VIJA CELMINS

PLATE 13   *DREAM BUILDING I,* 1979

STATEMENT

"Dream Building I" is the first work I made after the theft of my work dealing with the Ku Klux Klan. This occurred in January 1979 and "Dream Building I" was made in the spring of 1979.

I dreamed that I was driving down a back country road in Alabama, and before me was this building with no windows or doors, with a pitched roof. The building was covered with old outdoor advertising signs. The dream was so vivid that I decided to build what I had dreamed.

Most of the buildings I have made are based on literal structures, and I would like to be able to utilize the dream source, but of course I have no control of this.

Bill Christenberry, 1983

SELECTED BIOGRAPHY

Born in Tuscaloosa, Alabama, 1936
Lives in Washington, D.C.

Selected Honors
1983 Doctor of Fine Arts (honorary), Kansas City Art Institute, MO
1982 Lyndhurst Foundation Award
1976 National Endowment for the Arts, Artist's Fellowship

Commission
1978 U.S. General Services Administration, Art-in-Architecture Program: creation of a wall work ("Southern Wall") for the Federal Building, Jackson, MI

Selected Solo Exhibitions
1983- "William Christenberry/Southern Views," Rice Museum, Rice
82   University, Houston, TX (circulated: Corcoran Gallery of Art, Washington, D.C.; Huntsville Museum, AL [selected works])
1982   Middendorf/Lane Gallery, Washington, D.C.
       Morgan Gallery, Kansas City, KS
1980   Sander Gallery, Washington, D.C.
1979   The Montgomery Museum of Fine Arts, AL
1977   University Art Gallery, State University of New York, Albany, NY
1976   University of Alabama Art Gallery, Tuscaloosa, AL
1973   "Photographs by William Christenberry," The Octagon House, American Institute of Architects, Washington, D.C.

Selected Group Exhibitions
1983 "Contemporary Photographs from the Museum's Collection and Alfred Glassell School of Art HMFA 1983," KKKK, Houston, TX
      "The Southern Tradition: Five Southern Photographers—E.J. Bellocq, Clarence John Laughlin, Ralph Eugene Meatyard, William Christenberry, William Eggleston," Atlanta Gallery of Photography, TA
      "Trends in Color," The Focus Gallery, San Francisco, CA
1982 "William Christenberry, Robert Frank, Emmet Gowin, Clarence John Laughlin," Chrysler Museum of Art, Norfolk, VA
1981 "The Image of the House in Contemporary Art," University of Houston, Lawndale Annex, Houston, TX (cat.)
      "Photography: The Formalist Vision," Institute of Contemporary Art, University of Pennsylvania, Philadelphia, PA
      "Poetic Objects," Washington Project for the Arts, Washington, D.C.
      "Southern Eve, Southern Mind—A Photographic Inquiry," Memphis State University, TN (cat.)
      "Neon Fronts—Luminous Art for the Urban Landscape," Washington Project for the Arts, Washington, D.C.
      "An Invitational Exhibition of Monumental Art by Southern Artists," Memphis State University, TN
1980 "11th International Sculpture Conference," Washington, D.C.
      "Zeitgenossische Amerikanische Farbphotographie," Galerie Rudolf Kicken, Cologne, West Germany
      "Washington Photography in the Seventies—A Different Light," Washington Project for the Arts, Washington, D.C.
1979 "American Photography of the '70s," The Art Institute of Chicago, IL
      "Fotografie im Alltag Amerikas," Das Kunsigewerbemuseum, Zurich, Switzerland
1978 "Changing Prospects: Views of America on Paper," Corcoran Gallery of Art, Wahington, D.C.
      "Amerikanische Landschaftsphotographie," Neue Sammlung, Staatliches Museum für angewandte Kunst, Munich, West Germany (cat.)
      "Micro-Sculpture," Mandeville Art Gallery, University of California, San Diego, La Jolla, CA
1977 "10 Photographs contemporains/tendances actuelles aux Etats-Unis," Galerie Zabriskie, Paris, France
      "Five Years of Collecting Photographs," Yale University Art Gallery, New Haven, CT
      "Contemporary Color Photography—An Invitational Exhibit," Indiana University Art Museum, Bloomington, IN
      "William Christenberry—William Eggleston—Color Photographs," Morgan Gallery, Kansas City, KS
      "Points of View—101 Ways to Photograph a Tombstone or Make a Rubbing," The Center Gallery, University of California, Extension Center, San Francisco, CA
      "Bill Christenberry–Walker Evans–Photographs," Longwood Gallery, Massachusetts College of Art, Boston, MA
1976 "Spectrum," Rochester Institute of Technology, NY
      "52 Photographs by 52 Photographers, A Survey through the Medium," Sander Gallery, Washington, D.C.
      "Color Photographs 1976—Christenberry, Eggleston, Gossage, Myerowitz, Nixon, Shore," Broxton Gallery, Los Angeles, CA
1975 "Fourteen American Photographers," Baltimore Museum of Art, MD
      "Light/Sculpture," William Hayes Ackland Memorial Art Center, University of North Carolina, Chapel Hill, NC
      "Alabama Bag," Gallery 641, Washington, D.C.
1974 "Straight Color," Rochester Institute of Technology, NY
      "Seventeen Washington Artists, Where Has All the Color Gone?," Henri II Gallery, Washington, D.C.

WORKS IN THE EXHIBITION

"Coleman's Cafe I," 1982*
Building: 18⅜″ × 25¾″ × 36½″; base tray: 2¾″ × 36½″ × 49⅜″
Mixed media with red soil

"China Grove Memory," 1980*
Building: 17¼″ × 19⅛″ × 29″; base tray: 32″ × 37″ × 29″
Mixed media with red soil

"Dream Building I," 1979 (plate 13)
Building: 28⅞″ × 13″ × 13″; base tray: 2½″ × 18″ × 18″
Wood, balsa, paper, paint and Alabama soil
Lent by Edwin Janss
Photographed by Bob Grove

"Providence Church," 1975–76
Building: 22″ × 22⅛″ × 27¾″; base tray: 21″ × 72″ × 60″
Mixed media with tan soil

WILLIAM CHRISTENBERRY

PLATE 14   *EXTINGUISH ALL FLAMES*, 1980

STATEMENT

My interest in the house originated partly in a childhood preoccupation with building/making a "house" within the confines of my parents' home and partly out of an adult desire to explore specific polar states of being relevant to the structure and also to the personal psyche; i.e., open/closed, inside/outside, and adult/child.

Julie Cohn, 1983

SELECTED BIOGRAPHY
Born in Tulsa, Oklahoma, 1955
Lives in Dallas, Texas

Selected Honors
1980   Purchase Award, "23rd North Dakota Annual Print and Drawing Competition," University of North Dakota, Grand Forks, ND

Selected Solo Exhibitions
1983   DW Gallery, Dallas, TX
1982   Meadows Gallery, Southern Methodist University, Dallas, TX
1980   DW Gallery, Dallas, TX

Selected Group Exhibitions
1983   "Book/Art," The Signature Shop, Atlanta, GA
1981   "Mysterious Messages," Patrick Gallery, Austin, TX
       "New Figures," Hadler/Rodriguez Galleries, Houston, TX
       "The Image of the House in Contemporary Art," University of Houston, Lawndale Annex, TX (cat.)
1980   "Visions and Figurations," California State University, Fullerton, CA (cat.)
       "23rd North Dakota Annual Print and Drawing Competition," University of North Dakota, Grand Forks, ND
1979   "Group Show," Jas. K. Wilson Gallery, Dallas, TX
       "Women and Their Work," Austin, TX
       "Young American Printmakers," Clifford Gallery, Dallas, TX
       "Dallas Art '79," Dallas City Hall, TX (cat.)
       Cedar Valley Community College, Lancaster, TX
1978   "Annual Senior Exhibition," Kansas City Art Institute, MO
       "30 Miles of Art," Nelson Gallery of Art, Atkins Museum of Fine Arts, Kansas City, MO
       "Pictorial History of the World," Kansas City Art Institute Gallery, MO (cat.)

WORK IN THE EXHIBITION

"Extinguish All Flames," 1980 (plate 14)*
7'×6'×6,' wood and woodcut on paper
Photographed by Linda Finnell

41   JULIE COHN

PLATE 15   *TOURIST CABIN PORCH (MAINE)*, 1976

42

STATEMENT

For me, a building is like a person: the same basic structure, but altered, enriched over the years. I like buildings that show the passage of time, that look like they've lived a bit, that connect me with the past.

It has occurred to me that my interest in a kind of architecture generally cosidered unimportant—subway stations, tourist cabins—relates directly to my feminism. Focusing on these "humble" structures is for me very much like the feminist movement focusing on the lives of women and discovering there a whole world that was previously overlooked.

Donna Dennis, 1983

SELECTED BIOGRAPHY

Born in Springfield, Ohio, 1942
Lives in New York, New York

Selected Honors

1983 National Endowment for the Arts, Artist's Fellowship
1981 New York State Council on the Arts, Creative Artists Public Service Grant, Sculpture
1980 National Endowment for the Arts, Artist's Fellowship
1979 Guggenheim Fellowship
1977 National Endowment for the Arts, Artist's Fellowship
1975 New York State Council on the Arts, Creative Artists Public Service Grant, Painting

Selected Solo Exhibitions

1983 Holly Solomon Gallery, New York, NY
     Adler Gallery, Los Angeles, CA
1981 "Maquettes and Drawings," Locus Solus Gallery, Genoa, Italy
1980 "Donna Dennis," Sullivant Gallery, Ohio State University, Columbus, OH
     "New York and New Jersey," Holly Solomon Gallery, New York, NY
1979 "Three Sculptures by Donna Dennis," Contemporary Arts Center, Cincinnati, OH (cat.)
1978 "Maquettes and Drawings," Adler Gallery, Los Angeles, CA
     "Donna Dennis," Holly Solomon Gallery, New York, NY
1976 "Subway Stations and Tourist Cabins," Holly Solomon Gallery, New York, NY

Selected Site Works

1983 "River Resort," Mocassin Creek, Aberdeen, SD
1981 "Mad River Tunnel: Entrance and Exit," Dayton City Beautiful Program, OH (cat.)

Selected Group Exhibitions

1983 "Connections: Bridges/Ladders/Ramps/Staircases/Tunnels," Institute of Contemporary Art, University of Pennsylvania, Philadelphia, PA
     "Artists' Architecture," Institute of Contemporary Arts, London, England (cat.)
     "Painting and Sculpture by Candidates for Art Awards," American Academy and Institute of Arts and Letters Gallery, New York, NY
     "Ornamentalism: The New Decorativeness in Architecture and Design," The Hudson River Museum, Yonkers, NY
1982 "Aperto," Venice Biennale, Italy (cat.)
     "Contemporary Realism at One Penn Plaza," New York, NY
     "CAPS Sculptors," The Hudson River Museum, Yonkers, NY
     "Drawings by Contemporary Sculptors," Surrey Art Gallery, Surrey, British Columbia, Canada (circulated: University of Lethbridge Art Gallery, Alberta, Canada; London Regional Art Gallery, Ontario, Canada; Dalhousie Art Gallery, Halifax, Nova Scotia, Canada; Sir George Williams Galleries, Montreal, Quebec, Canada) (cat.)
     "Skowhegan Faculty Show," Colby College, Waterville, ME
     "New York Now," Kestner-Gesellschaft, Hannover, West Germany (circulated: Kunstverein, Munich, West Germany; Musee Cantonal des Beaux-Arts, Lausanne, France; Kunstverein für die Rheinlande und Westfalen, Dusseldorf, West Germany (cat.)

"Houses," Sculpture Center, New York, NY
1981 "The Image of the House in Contemporary Art," University of Houston, Lawndale Annex, TX (cat.)
     "Developments in Recent Sculpture," Whitney Museum of American Art, New York, NY (cat.)
     "The Soft Land—Il Soffice Paese," Palazzo Farnese, Ortona, Italy (cat.)
     "Aspects of Post-Modernism: Decorative and Narrative Art," The Squibb Gallery, Princeton, NJ (cat.)
     "Homework: The Domestic Environment Reflected in the Work of Contemporary Women Artists," Women's Hall of Fame, Seneca Falls, NY (circulated: Joe and Emily Lowe Art Gallery, Syracuse University, NY; The Henry Street Settlement House, New York, NY (cat.)
1980 "Les Nouveaux Fauves—Die Neuen Wilden," Neue Galerie–Sammlung Ludwig, Aachen, West Germany (cat.)
     "Architectural Sculpture," Los Angeles Institute of Contemporary Art (Downtown), CA (cat.)
     "Tableau: An American Selection," Middendorf/Lane Gallery, Washington, D.C. (cat.)
     "The Whitney Biennial Exhibition of Painting and Sculpture," Whitney Museum of American Art, New York, NY (cat.)
     "Directions," Hirshhorn Museum and Sculpture Garden, Smithsonian Institution, Washington, D.C. (cat.)
1978 "Dwellings," Institute of Contemporary Art, University of Pennsylvania, Philadelphia, PA (circulated: Neuberger Museum, State University of New York, College at Purchase, NY) (cat.)

WORKS IN THE EXHIBITION

"Subway with Silver Girders," 1982*
12' × 12'2" × 14,' mixed media

"Two Stories with Porch," 1977-79*
10'6" × 10'½" × 7,' mixed media

"Tourist Cabin Porch (Maine)," 1976 (plate 15)
6'6½" × 6'10" × 2'2½," mixed media
Photograph by Bevan Davies, courtesy of Holly Solomon Gallery, New York, NY

"Subway Station with Yellow and Blue," 1974–76*
6'7" × 4'1" × 5'5½," mixed media

43

DONNA DENNIS

PLATE 16   *LAND STRUCTURES BUILT WHERE THE PETROGLYPHS ARE MADE BY CHILDREN, 1977*

44

STATEMENT

Harriet Feigenbaum's polygonal dwellings and fence pieces are parts of a continuing *Cycles* series. They are made of natural saplings and branches, but bound together with wire as an intentionally intrusive "modern" element. Once entered, these openwork shelters separate but do not close off the site. The sky is visible through the graphic screen of the dome; the environment is visible through the walls. One is both inside and outside, contained but not contained.

Feigenbaum has long been interested in distance (cultural and physical) and how it is affected by the contours of the land; and in balance and natural movement. . . . She is a contemporary urban artist exploiting relics from slower times. Feigenbaum's "primitivism" is particularly interesting because it rejects escapism to the past by juxtaposition with existing structures—architectural and social. Instead, one culture is invaded by another. . . ."

From Lucy R. Lippard, "Complexes: Architecture in Nature," *Art in America*, January-February 1979, p. 96.

SELECTED BIOGRAPHY

Born in New York, New York, 1939
Lives in New York, New York

Selected Honors
1983 Plaza design for Battery Park City Commercial Center, New York, NY; invited by Cesar Pelli, Dean, Yale University School of Architecture, New Haven, CT
Scranton Area Foundation, PA
1982 Pennsylvania Council on the Arts, PA
1977 America the Beautiful Fund, Washington, D.C.
New York State Council on the Arts, Creative Artists Public Service Grant
1961 Hallgarten Fellowship, National Academy of Design, NY

Selected Solo Exhibitions
1983 Lackawanna County Courthouse, Scranton, PA
1981 Marian Locks Gallery, Philadelphia, PA
1976 City University Graduate Center Mall, New York, NY
1974 Warren Benedek Gallery, New York, NY
Spook Farm Gallery, Far Hills, NJ
1972 Warren Benedek Gallery, New York, NY
1969 Ruth White Gallery, New York, NY

Selected Site Work in Progress
1983- Reclamation of sixty acres of strip mine spoils, serpentine vine-
80   yard and complementary pine forest, Route U.S. 6, Dickson City, PA (anticipated completion 1985)

European Site Works
1976 "The Structuring of Barren Ground," Olmastrino Farm, Greve, Italy
1974 "Hayricks Until the August Fires," Torre al Pino, Molino del Piano, Italy
1973 "Windricks in the Mistral at Mas de S. Jerome," Laussane, France
1971 "Hay Structures on the Farm of Duke and Duchess Salviati," Migliarino Pisano, Italy
1969 "The Gates of Cinaglio," Cinaglio, Italy

Selected Group Exhibitions
1980 "Architectural Sculpture," Los Angeles Institute of Contemporary Art, CA (cat.)
"Breaking In," Creative Time, Inc., New York, NY
"Drawings III," Touchstone Gallery, New York, NY
1980, "Transformations to an Inner Island Village," Ward's Island, New
79,78 York, NY
1979 "Aspects of Childhood: Sources in Recent American Art/Architecture," New Jersey Institute of Technology, School of Architecture, Newark, NJ

"Lines, Points, Planes," Roosevelt Museum, NY
"Estuary," Merce Cunningham Studio, New York, NY (commissioned for Simone Forti)
1978 "The Presence of Nature," Whitney Museum of American Art, New York, NY
"Dwellings," Institute of Contemporary Art, University of Pennsylvania, Philadelphia, PA (circulated: Neuberger Museum, State University of New York, College at Purchase, NY) (cat.)
"Art on the Beach," Creative Time, Inc., New York, NY
"Artyard," The Brooklyn Museum, NY
O.K. Harris Gallery, New York, NY
1977 ArtPark, Lewiston, NY
"Women in American Architecture: A Historic and Contemporary Perspective," The Brooklyn Museum, NY (circulated: Hayden Gallery, Massachusetts Institute of Technology, Cambridge, MA; Colorado Springs Fine Arts Center, CO)
"Contemporary Landscape: Image and Idea," Queensborough Community College, Bayside, NY
1976 "Sculpture Sited," Nassau County Museum of Fine Arts, Roslyn, NY
1975 "Works on Paper," The Brooklyn Museum, NY
1974 "Fiftieth Anniversary of Surrealism," French Cultural Services, New York, NY
1973 "New York Artists on Tour, Sculpture-3," New York City Department of Cultural Affairs, NY
"New York Today—Works on Paper," University of Missouri, St. Louis, MO
1972 "Young Artists," Warren Benedek Gallery, New York, NY
1971 "Sculpture," Hundred Acres Gallery, New York, NY
1967 "66 Grippi Gallery, New York, NY

WORKS IN THE EXHIBITION

"Land Structures Built Where the Petroglyphs are Made by Children," 1977 (plate 16)*
Five structures, each 12'–15' × 16' diameter, built on five acres; wood, wire and stone
ArtPark, Lewiston, NY
Photographed by Andrew Strout

"Parking Lot Pentagon Off Washington Avenue," 1978*
Fence: 5' × 5' × 154'; building: 10' × 13' diameter; logs and wire
The Brooklyn Museum, NY

"Battery Park City—A Mirage," 1978*
10' × 100' diameter; branches, driftwood and wire
"Art on the Beach," New York, NY

45 HARRIET FEIGENBAUM

PLATE 17   *RECALL*, 1980

46

STATEMENT

My work is primarily about—

1. the process of building form,

2. internal and external rhythms derived from—

   a. the inherent structure (counter-positioning of end grains),

   b. "drawing" on the surface (spacing which produces gaps and/or slats of light,

3. a look of timelessness so the pieces can sit comfortably, but not specifically, in any time period—whether the past, present or future.

Jackie Ferrara, 1983

SELECTED BIOGRAPHY

Born in Detroit, Michigan
Lives in New York, New York

Selected Solo Exhibitions

1983 Max Protetch Gallery, New York, NY
      University of North Carolina, Chapel Hill, NC
      Janus Gallery, Los Angeles, CA
      Galleriet, Lund, Sweden
1982 Max Protetch Gallery, New York, NY
      Lowe Art Museum, Coral Gables, FL
1981 Max Protetch Gallery, New York, NY
      Laumeier Sculpture Park Gallery, St. Louis, MO
      Marianne Deson Gallery, Chicago, IL
1980 Okun-Thomas Gallery, St. Louis, MO
      University of Massachusetts, Amherst, MA (circulated: San Francisco Art Institute, CA; University of Southern California, Los Angeles, CA) (cat.)
1979 University of Rhode Island, Kingston, RI
      Glen Hanson Gallery, Minneapolis, MN
      Max Protetch Gallery, New York, NY
1978 The Minneapolis College of Art and Design, MN
      Max Protetch Gallery, New York, NY
1977 Ohio State University, Columbus, OH
      Max Protetch Gallery, Washington, D.C.
1976, Max Protetch Gallery, New York, NY
75
1975 Max Protetch Gallery, Washington, D.C.
      Daniel Weinberg Gallery, San Francisco, CA
1974, A.M. Sachs Gallery, New York, NY
73

Selected Site Works

1982 Neuberger Museum, State University of New York, College at Purchase, NY
1981 Laumeier Sculpture Park, St. Louis, MO
1980 Wave Hill, Riverdale, NY (cat.)
      Federal Building, Carbondale, IL
1979 Castle Clinton, Battery Park, New York, NY (cat.)
1978 The Minneapolis College of Art and Design, MN
      City Beautiful Council, Dayton, OH
1976 Dag Hammarskjöld Plaza, New York, NY
1973 Storm King Art Center, Mountainville, NY

Selected Group Exhibitions

1983 "Michele Stuart and Jackie Ferrara," Janus Gallery, Los Angeles, CA
1982 "Objects into Structures," University of South Florida, Tampa, FL
1981 "The Image of the House in Contemporary Art," University of Houston, Lawndale Annex, TX (cat.)
      "Group Show," Okin-Thomas Gallery, St. Louis, MO
      "Architecture by Artists," Rosa Esman Gallery, New York, NY
      "30 Years of Public Sculpture in Illinois," Lakeview Museum of Arts and Sciences, Peoria, IL

"Currents, Trends for the '80s," Jacksonville Art Museum, FL
"A Range of Contemporary Drawing," Wilkes College, Wilkes-Barre, PA
"Drawing Acquisitions 1978-81," Whitney Museum of American Art, New York, NY
"Sculpture Invitational," Zabriskie Gallery, New York, NY
1980 "Intricate Structure/Repeated Image," Tyler School of Art, Philadelphia, PA
      "Drawings: The Pluralist Decade," Venice Biennale, Italy (circulated: Institute of Contemporary Art, University of Pennsylvania, Philadelphia, PA; Museum of Contemporary Art, Chicago, IL) (cat.)
      "11th International Sculpture Conference," Washington, D.C.
      "Painting and Sculpture Today 1980," Indianapolis Museum of Art, IN
      "Across the Nation, Fine Art for Federal Buildings, 1972-1979," National Collection of Fine Arts, Smithsonian Institution, Washington, D.C.
      "Architectural Sculpture," Los Angeles Institute of Contemporary Art, CA (cat.)
      "Woodworks I: New American Sculpture," Dayton Art Institute, OH
      "Sculpture at the Coliseum," New York Coliseum, NY
1979 "Art and Architecture, Space and Structure," Protetch-McIntosh Gallery, Washington, D.C.
      "The Minimal Tradition," Aldrich Museum of Contemporary Art, Ridgefield, CT
      "Castle Clinton: Interpretations '79," Battery Park, New York, NY
1978 "Indoor-Outdoor," P.S. 1, The Institute for Art and Urban Resources, Long Island City, NY
      "Architectural Analogues," Whitney Museum Downtown Branch, New York, NY (cat.)
1977 "Ferrara, Lichtenstein, Nevelson, Ryman," Sarah Lawrence College, Bronxville, NY (cat.)
      "Works and Projects of the Seventies," P.S. 1, The Institute for Art and Urban Resources, Long Island City, NY
1976 "New York–Downtown Manhattan: Soho," Berlin Festival, Akademie der Kunst, West Germany
1974 "Seven Sculptors," Institute of Contemporary Art, Boston, MA
      "Painting and Sculpture Today 1974," Indianapolis Museum of Art, IN (circulated: Contemporary Arts Center, Cincinnati, OH)
1973 "The Whitney Biennial Exhibition of Painting and Sculpture," Whitney Museum of American Art, New York, NY
1972 "GEDOK American Women Artist Show," Kunsthaus, Hamburg, West Germany
1970 "Annual Exhibition of Contemporary American Sculpture," Whitney Museum of American Art, New York, NY

WORKS IN THE EXHIBITION

"Laumeier Project," 1981*
16'4" × 21'8" × 19,' cedar
Site: St. Louis, MO

"Recall," 1980 (plate 17)*
76½" × 37½" × 37½," pine
Courtesy of Janus Gallery, Los Angeles, CA
Photographed by Roy M. Elkind

"I-15 Ramp," 1974*
11¼" × 71¼" × 23¼," chipboard

JACKIE FERRARA

PLATE 18 *UNTITLED*, 1981

48

STATEMENT

But if we are ever to have a bearable sculpture or architecture it might be well for young sculptors to start with some such effort at perfection, rather than with the idea of a new Laocoon, or a "Triumph of Labour over Commerce." (This suggestion is mine, and I hope it will never fall under the eye of Brancusi. —But then Brancusi can spend most of his time in his own studio, surrounded by the calm of his own creations, whereas the author of this imperfect exposure is compelled to move about in a world full of junk-shops, a world full of more than idiotic ornamentations, a world where pictures are made for museums, where no man has a front-door that he can bear to look at, let alone one he can contemplate with reasonable pleasure, where the average house is each year made more hideous, and where the sense of form which ought to be the pleasure of liquid in time of drouth or any other clear animal pleasure, is the rare possession of an "intellectual" (heaven help us) "aristocracy."

From Ezra Pound, "The Little Review," Autumn 1921, pp. 3-7, in *Literary Essays* (New York and London, 1954), pp. 441-45.

SELECTED BIOGRAPHY
Born in New York, New York, 1944
Lives in Providence, Rhode Island

Selected Honors
1981- National Endowment for the Arts, Artist's Fellowship
80
1976- National Endowment for the Arts, Artist's Fellowship
75
1975- Grant-in-Aid, Rhode Island State Council on the Arts
74
1973, Summer stipend, Brown University, Providence, RI, building of
72,71 earth works

Selected Solo Exhibitions
1981, Max Protetch Gallery, New York, NY
80
1980 Museum of Art, Rhode Island School of Design, Providence, RI
1977 University Gallery, University of Massachusetts, Amherst, MA
1976 Hammarskjold Plaza, New York, NY
1975, Terry Dintenfass Gallery, New York, NY
73,71
1971 Hopkins Art Center, Dartmouth College, Hanover, NH

Selected Site Works
1980 "Wood Interior," Museum of Art, Rhode Island School of Design, Providence, RI
"Baltimore Project," Woodlawn, MD
1980- "Fence/Covered Fence," XIII Winter Olympic Games, Lake
79 Placid, NY
1979- "Chain Link Maze," University of Massachusetts, Amherst, MA
78 "Sites Resited," Dayton, OH, and Wright State University, Dayton, OH
1977 "Floating Square," Kassel, West Germany
1977- "Cow Island Project," Roger Williams Park, Providence, RI
76
1976 "Sod Drawing," Roger Sherman Baldwin Park, Greenwich, CT
"Sited Works," Nassau County Museum of Fine Arts, Roslyn, NY
"Sod Construction," Hammarskjold Plaza, New York, NY
1975 "Sod Drawing," Far Hills, NJ
1974 "Sod Maze," Chateau-sur'Mer, Newport, RI
1973 "Tufa Maze," Pocanto Hills, NY
1972 "Bluff," Rehoboth, MA
"Zig Zag," Rehoboth, MA
1971 "Hay Interior," Rehoboth, MA
"Hay Line," Rehoboth, MA

Selected Group Exhibitions
1983 "Sculpture as Architecture," Thomas Segal Gallery, Boston, MA
1981 "Artists Make Architecture," Rosa Esman Gallery, New York, NY
"The Image of the House in Contemporary Art," University of Houston, Lawndale Annex, TX (cat.)
1980 Four Olympic Commissions, Max Protetch Gallery, New York, NY
"Architectural Sculpture," Los Angeles Institute of Contemporary Art, CA (cat.)
"Drawings/Structures, Institute of Contemporary Art," Boston, MA
"Drawings: The Pluralist Decade, 39th Venice Biennale," Italy (circulated: Institute of Contemporary Art, University of Pennsylvania, Philadelphia, PA; Museum of Contemporary Art, Chicago, IL) (cat.)
"Arts on the Line, Art for Public Transit Spaces," Hayden Gallery, Massachusetts Institute of Technology, Cambridge, MA
1976- "Labyrinths," Wheaton College, Norton, MA (circulated: Philadelphia College of Art, PA; Corcoran Gallery of Art, Washington, D.C.)
75
1975 "Projects in Nature," Far Hills, NJ
"Boston Bicentennial Art Collection," Institute of Contemporary Art, Boston, MA
1974 "Awards Exhibition," The American Academy of Arts and Letters and the National Institute of Arts and Letters, New York, NY

WORKS IN THE EXHIBITION

"Untitled," modular block construction, 1981 (plate 18, cat. only)
22'7 1/16" × 11'5/8" × 8'7 1/4," particle board (to be constructed in stone)
Photographed by Gene Dwiggins

"Wood Interior," 1980*
17' × 62' × 34,' wood
Site: Museum of Art, Providence, RI

"Chain Link Maze," 1978*
8' × 5'1" × 5'1," chain link fencing
Site: Amherst, MA

RICHARD FLEISCHNER

PLATES 19, 20, 21 AND 22   *SNOW TREE HOUSE (FOUR VIEWS)*, 1980

STATEMENT

I and a few helpers built plywood forms to enclose the small stand of evergreens that were to serve as the corner posts of the piece. At Mirror Lake, the City was clearing a skating area of what little snow had fallen and answered my request to dump it all around the formed-in trees. A highway snow blower was then secured to drive the same circular path. It sucked up chunks of snow and spit a fine white powder into the formwork. After a day, the sintered snow settled and hardened enough to allow removal of the forms. What emerged was a crisp and sparkling monolith, like a newly sawn block of quarry granite. I began cutting with a snow shovel and finished, three days later, with a hatchet.

There was a directness in this approach that reminded me of igloo-building and rammed earth construction. All three share low technology, labor intensity and reliance on indigenous materials.

"Snow Tree House" stood alone yet integrated in its environment. It was an image of solitary dwelling adjacent to a resort hotel with standing room only. The way up—a confining, twisted, icy stair/passage—opened onto an intimate terrace at branch level among the tree. It was a difficult path to a new perspective.

Lloyd Hamrol, 1983

SELECTED BIOGRAPHY
Born in San Francisco, California, 1937
Lives in Venice, California

Selected Honors
1980   National Endowment for the Arts, Artist's Fellowship
1974   National Endowment for the Arts, Artist's Fellowship
1965   New Talent Purchase Award, Contemporary Arts Council, Los Angeles County Museum of Art, CA

Selected Solo Exhibitions
1970   Installation, California State University, Fullerton, CA
1969   Installation, Pomona College, CA
1968   Installation, La Jolla Museum of Art, CA

Selected Site Works
1983   "Flagstone Ramp," Fountain Valley, CA
       "City Terrace," Anaheim, CA
       "Squaredance," California State University, Long Beach, CA
1982   "Rockwalls," Gallaudet College, Washington, D.C.
1980   "Rock Creek Project," Rock Creek Park, Washington, D.C.
       "Highground," School of Law, University of New Mexico, Albuquerque, NM
1979   "Thronapolis," The Russell Federal Building, Atlanta, GA
       "Gyrojack," The Regrade Park, Seattle, WA
1977   "Redoubling Wallpath," California State University, Fullerton, CA
1975   "L.A. Roxhole," Los Angeles, CA, private collection
1974   "Log Ramps," Western Washington University, Bellingham, WA
1973   "Woven Cone," California Institute of the Arts, Valencia, CA

Site Works in Progress
Harborview Development Center, Valdez, AK
City of Monterey, CA
Exposition Park, Los Angeles, CA
University of Iowa, Iowa City, IA

Selected Group Exhibitions
1983   "Young Talent Awards: 1963-1983," Los Angeles County Museum of Art, CA (cat.)
       "The Place of Art in Public Places," Allegheny Bureau of Cultural Programs, Pittsburgh, PA
1981   "Art in Los Angeles—The Museum as Site: Sixteen Projects," Los Angeles County Museum of Art, CA (cat.)
1980   "Across the Nation: Fine Art for Federal Buildings, 1972-79," National Collection of Fine Arts, Smithsonian Institution, Washington, D.C. (circulated: Hunter Museum of Art, Chattanooga, TN)
       "Architectural Sculpture," Municipal Art Gallery, Barnsdall Park, Los Angeles, CA (organized by Los Angeles Institute of Contemporary Art, CA) (cat.)
       XIII Olympic Winter Games, Lake Placid, NY
       "11th International Sculpture Conference," Washington, D.C.
       "Urban Encounters/Art Architecture Audience," Institute of Contemporary Art, University of Pennsylvania, Philadelphia, PA
       "Sculpture in California 1975–80," San Diego Museum of Art, CA
1979- "Los Angeles in the Seventies," Fort Worth Art Museum, TX
77   (circulated: Joslyn Art Museum, Omaha, NB)
1977- "Painting and Sculpture in California: The Modern Era," San
76   Francisco Museum of Modern Art, CA (circulated: National Collection of Fine Art, Smithsonian Institution, Washington, D.C.)
       "16 Projects/4 Artists: Siah Armajani, Larry Bell, Lloyd Hamrol, Pat Steir," Court House Square, Dayton, OH (circulated: Moore College of Art, Philadelphia, PA; University of Kentucky, Lexington, KY) (cat.)
1977, "Site Sculpture," Zabriskie Gallery, New York, NY
75
1976   "ArtPark, Lewiston, NY
1975   "Three L.A. Sculptors," Los Angeles Institute of Contemporary Art, CA
1974   "Public Sculpture/Urban Environment," The Oakland Museum, CA
1973   "Four Los Angeles Sculptors," Museum of Contemporary Art, Chicago, IL
1972   "15 Los Angeles Artists," Pasadena Museum of Modern Art, CA
1972   "Allen Bertoldi and Lloyd Hamrol," California State University,
1971   Fresno, CA
1970   "String and Rope," Sidney Janis Gallery, New York, NY
1969   "Invisible Painting and Sculpture," Richmond Art Center, CA
1968   "West Coast Now," Portland Museum of Art, OR (circulated: Seattle Museum of Art, WA; Municipal Art Gallery, Barnsdall Park, Los Angeles, CA; San Francisco Museum of Art, CA)
1967   "American Sculpture of the Sixties," Los Angeles County Museum of Art, CA (circulated: Philadelphia Museum of Art, PA)
1966   "Annual Exhibition of Contemporary American Sculpture and Prints," Whitney Museum of American Art, New York, NY

WORK IN THE EXHIBITION

"Snow Tree House" (four views), 1980 (plates 19, 20, 21 and 22)*
16' × 16' × 20,' cast pulverized snow
Site: XIII Winter Olympic Games, Lake Placid, NY
Photographed by Lloyd Hamrol

LLOYD HAMROL

PLATE 23   *STONE ENCLOSURE: ROCK RINGS, 1977–78*

52

STATEMENT

Often when people enter my work I have the sensation that they are going right through me, reverberating in a tunnel through my heart, "seen from the inside, without exteriority, being can only be round" (Gaston Bachelard).

These enclosures draw people in, but once inside they offer views of the outside world. There is no easy peace at the center, only a desire to be in when out and out when in.

> We pierce doors and windows to make a house;
> And it is on these spaces where there is nothing that
>   the usefulness of the house depends. . . .
>   (Tao Tê Ching)

At times the openings in the works can be like eyes in space, or they can be the points of passage from one state to another—dark/light, in/out, birth/death.

Nancy Holt, 1983

SELECTED BIOGRAPHY

Born in Worcester, Massachusetts, 1938
Lives in New York, New York

Selected Honors

1983 National Endowment for the Arts, Artist's Fellowship
1978 National Endowment for the Arts, Artist's Fellowship
New York State Council on the Arts, Creative Artists Public Service Grant, Video
Guggenheim Fellowship, Sculpture
1977 WNET-Channel 13 Artist-in-Residence Grant
Beard's Fund, Inc.
1975 National Endowment for the Arts, Artist's Fellowship
New York State Council on the Arts, Creative Artists Public Service Grant, Sculpture

Selected Solo Exhibitions

1982 John Weber Gallery, New York, NY
David Bellman Gallery, Toronto, Ontario, Canada
1981 Saginaw Art Museum, MI
1979 John Weber Gallery, New York, NY
Miami University Art Center, Oxford, OH
1977 Franklin Furnace, New York, NY
1974 Bykert Gallery, New York, NY
Walter Kelly Gallery, Chicago, IL
1973 Lo Guidice Gallery, New York, NY
1972 Art Gallery, University of Montana, Missoula, MT
Art Center, University of Rhode Island, Kingston, RI

Selected Film and Video

1982 "A Space," Toronto, Ontario, Canada
1980 "Cinemateque," San Francisco, CA
Film Section, Carnegie Institute, Pittsburg, PA
1979 The Museum of Modern Art, New York, NY
1978 "Sun Tunnels," 16mm, color and sound, 26 minutes (film)
1977 "Revolve," black and white, 75 minutes
1975 "Pine Barrens," 16mm, color and sound, 32 minutes (film)
1974 "Underscan," black and white, 8 minutes
"Points of View," The Clocktower, New York, NY
1973 "Going Around in Circles," black and white, 15 minutes
"Xeroing In," black and white, 28 minutes
1972 "Locating #1 and #2," black and white, 15 minutes each
1969 "East Coast–West Coast," black and white, 20 minutes (with Robert Smithson)

Selected Site Works

1983 "Sole Source," Marlay Park, Dublin, Ireland
"Waterwork," Gallaudet College, Washington, D.C. (in progress)
"Astral Grating," IRT subway, Fulton Street, New York, NY (in progress)
1982 "Catch Basin," St. James Park, King and Jarvis Streets, Toronto, Ontario, Canada
1981 "Time Span," Laguna Gloria Museum, Austin, TX
1980-79 "Wild Spot," Wellesley College, MA
1978-77 "Stone Enclosure: Rock Rings," Western Washington University, Bellingham, WA
1976-73 "Sun Tunnels," northwest Utah desert, four miles southeast of Lucin, UT
1974 "Hydra's Head," along the Niagara River, Lewiston, NY
1972 "Views through a Sand Dune," Narragansett Beach, RI
"Missoula Ranch Locators," twenty-two miles north of Missoula, MT

Selected Group Exhibitions

1983 "Art of the '60s," P.S. 1, The Institute for Art and Urban Resources, New York, NY
"Artists' Books and Documents," Wallace Memorial Library Galleries, Rochester Institute of Technology, NY
"Artists as Filmmakers," A.I.R. Gallery, New York, NY
"Video Around Town," organized by 185 Nassau Street Corporation at Just Above Midtown/Downtown Gallery, New York; Port Authority Bus Terminal, New York; John F. Kennedy Airport, New York; Kings Plaza Mall, Brooklyn; Astoria Studios, Queens ("Underscan"), NY
"Independent Artists Open Air Sculpture Exhibition," Marlay Park, Dublin, Ireland (organized by Douglas Hyde Gallery, Trinity College, Dublin, Ireland)
"Women Sculptors' Drawings," Max Hutchinson Gallery, New York, NY
"Views by Women Artists," 16 Independent Exhibitions, New York, NY
"Citysite Sculpture: Starting Line," Market Gallery, Toronto, Ontario, Canada
1981 "Artists' Gardens and Parks," Hayden Gallery, Massachusetts Institute of Technology, Cambridge, MA
"The Whitney Biennial Exhibition of Painting and Sculpture," Whitney Museum of American Art, New York, NY
"Natur-Skulptur/Nature-Sculpture," Wurttenbergischer Kunstverein, Stuttgart, West Germany
1980 1980 "Aspects of the Seventies: Sitework," Wellesley College, MA
"11th International Sculpture Conference," Washington, D.C.
"Architectural Sculpture," Los Angeles Institute of Contemporary Art, CA (cat.)
1979 "The Whitney Biennial Exhibition of Painting and Sculpture," Whitney Museum of American Art, New York, NY
1977 "Probing the Earth: Contemporary Land Projects," Hirshhorn Museum and Sculpture Garden, Smithsonian Institution, Washington, D.C.

WORKS IN THE EXHIBITION

"30 Below," 1979 *
30' x 9'4," bricks, earth and grass
Site: XIII Winter Olympic Games, Lake Placid, NY

"Stone Enclosure: Rock Rings," 1977–78 (plate 23)*
10' x 40' x 40' diameter, stone masonry
Site: Western Washington University, Bellingham, WA
Photographed by Nancy Holt

NANCY HOLT

PLATE 24   *THE FIFTH UTOPIA (FOR LEO)*, 1982

STATEMENT

Theater imagery has always been central to Johnson's work. "Theaters give me a great sense of anticipation," he says, "they seem like an entrance to the future."[1] His theaters consist of shadow box constructions which, whether replete with extraordinary authentic architectural detail or laden with fantastic embellishments, evoke a sense of intrigue which is theatrical in itself.

Suspense is inherent in the fact that one sees only a facade or, at most, a glimpse of an interior that does not supply an explanation. Looking at one of Johnson's theater boxes is very much like watching the curtain from a box within a theater; one has the feeling that much is taking place out of sight, and that it will be revealed at any moment.

The artist's recent work combines many of the sources that he has drawn upon in the past. Egyptian and Islamic architecture, classical sculpture, elements of ancient and medieval theater, and the "razzle-dazzle" of contemporary entertainment work together to create the effect of a personal nostalgia.

The buildings represented are no longer restricted specifically to theaters, but the dramatic aura remains.

Human absence is conspicuous in Johnson's buildings, leaving the viewer to wonder at the ghostly loneliness of a structure which is illuminated for no one. At question here is the "gravity and stability" of life.[2]

SELECTED BIOGRAPHY

Born in Elizabeth, New Jersey, 1941
Lives in upstate New York

Selected Solo Exhibitions

1981 Ace Gallery, Vancouver, British Columbia, Canada
Ace Gallery, Los Angeles, CA
1980 Leo Castelli Gallery, New York, NY
1976 The Arts Club of Chicago, IL
A.M. Sachs Gallery, New York, NY
1975 Neuberger Museum, State University of New York, College at Purchase, NY
1974 A.M. Sachs Gallery, New York, NY

Selected Group Exhibitions

1983 "Habitats," The Clocktower, The Institute for Art and Urban Resources, New York, NY
1982 "Artists Choose Artists," CDS Gallery, New York, NY
"Castelli and His Artists: Twenty-five Years" (circulated: La Jolla Museum of Contemporary Art, CA; Aspen Center for the Visual Arts, CO (exhibition organizer); Leo Castelli Gallery, New York, NY; Portland Center for the Visual Arts, OR; Laguna Gloria Art Museum, Austin, TX)
"Homage to Joseph Cornell," Gabrielle Bryers, New York, NY
"Selections from the Collection," Neuberger Museum, State University of New York, College at Purchase, NY
1980 "Spoleto Festival," Charleston, NC
"Architectural Sculpture," Los Angeles Institute of Contemporary Art, CA (cat.)
"Drawings to Benefit the Foundation for Contemporary Performance Arts, Inc.," Leo Castelli Gallery, New York, NY
1976 "Artworks," Milwaukee, WI
1975 "34th Society for Contemporary Art Exhibition," The Art Institute of Chicago, IL
"Collectors Choice XV," Philbrook Art Center, Tulsa, OK
"Spring Purchase Group," Weatherspoon Art Gallery, University of North Carolina, Greensboro, NC
1974 "New Talent Festival," A.M. Sachs Gallery, New York, NY
"Art on Paper," Weatherspoon Art Gallery, University of North Carolina, Greensboro, NC

WORKS IN THE EXHIBITION

"The Fifth Utopia (for Leo)," 1982 (plate 24)
33" × 31¼" × 11," mixed media
Lent by Leo Castelli
Photograph courtesy of Leo Castelli Gallery, New York, NY

"The Crescent," 1980*
49¼" × 37" × 12," mixed media

"Niobe," 1980*
25½" × 19½" × 11," mixed media

CLETUS JOHNSON

PLATES 25 AND 26   *THE BEANERY (TWO VIEWS)*, 1965

STATEMENT

"The Beanery" is a recreation of a famous old Los Angeles bar. It has been described elsewhere as a "communal coffin"—a sanctuary where alcohol lessens social barriers, many things are possible, and people escape to relax and "kill time." Time to Kienholz represents each individual's space before death, and this preoccupation with time and death can be seen as the fundamental basis of all his large environments. "The Beanery" assaults all the senses (except taste) with an intensified super-reality that demands response from all who enter its swinging doors.

From Pontus Hulten in *11 + 11 Tableaux*, January 17–March 1, 1970, Moderna Museet, Stockholm, Sweden

SELECTED BIOGRAPHY

Born in Fairfield, Washington, 1927
Lives in Hope, Idaho, and West Berlin, West Germany

Selected Solo Exhibitions
1981   The Douglas Hyde Gallery, Trinity College, Dublin, Ireland (cat.)
         Galerie Maeght, Zurich, Switzerland
1980   Gemini G.E.L., Los Angeles, CA
1979   Galerie Maeght, Paris, France (cat.)
         Louisiana Museum, Humlebaek, Denmark
         Henry Art Gallery, University of Washington, Seattle, WA
         University Art Museum, University of California, Berkeley, CA
1978   Akademie der Künste, West Berlin, West Germany
1977   Nationalgalerie, West Berlin, West Germany (circulated: Galerie Maeght, Zurich, Switzerland)
         Galleria d'Arte il Gabbiano, Rome, Italy (cat.)
         Centre National d'Arte et de Culture Georges Pompidou, Paris, France (cat.)
         Städtische Kunsthalle, Düsseldorf, West Germany
         Galerie Apollon Die Insel, Munich, West Germany
1974   Galerie Christel, Helsinki, Finland
         Galleria Bocchi, Milan, Italy (cat.)
         Akademie der Künste, West Berlin, West Germany
1973   Städtische Kunsthalle, Düsseldorf, West Germany
         Onnasch Gallery, Cologne, West Germany
1972   Gemini G.E.L., Los Angeles, CA
1972, Wide White Space Gallery, Antwerp, Belgium
71,70
1970   Onnasch Gallery, Cologne, West Germany
         Moderna Museet, Stockholm, Sweden (circulated: Stedelijk Museum, Amsterdam, The Netherlands; Städtische Kunsthalle, Düsseldorf, West Germany; Kunsthaus Zurich, Switzerland; The Museum of Modern Art, New York, NY; Centre National d'Art Contemporain, Paris, France; Institute of Contemporary Arts, London, England)
         Gallery Michael Werner, Cologne, West Germany
         Eugenia Butler Gallery, Los Angeles, CA
1969   Ateneumin Taidemuseo, Helsinki, Finland

Selected Group Exhibitions
1981   "The Whitney Biennial Exhibition of Painting and Sculpture," Whitney Museum of American Art, New York, NY
1980   "Ecouter par les veux," Musée d'Art Moderne de la Ville de Paris, France (cat.)
1978   "Aspekte der 60er Jahre: Aus der Sammlung Reinhard Onnasch," Nationalgalerie, West Berlin, West Germany (cat.)
1977   "Venice Biennale," Italy
1977- "Painting and Sculpture in California: The Modern Era," San
76   Francisco Museum of Modern Art, CA (circulated: National Collection of Fine Arts, Smithsonian Institution, Washington, D.C.)
1975   "8 from Berlin: Erben, Erber, Gosewitz, Hödicke, Kienholz, Koberling, Lakner, Schönebeck," Fruit Market Gallery, Scottish Arts Council, Edinburgh, Scotland
1974   "Ars 74," Ateneumin Taidemuseo, Helsinki, Finland
         "Word Works," Mt. San Antonio College, Walnut, CA
1972   "Dokumenta 4," Kassel, West Germany
1971   "Continuing Surrealism," La Jolla Museum of Contemporary Art, CA
         "Metamorphose van het Object," Musées Royaux des Beaux-Arts, Brussels, Belgium

1970   "Looking West 1970," Joslyn Art Museum, Omaha, NB
         "Das Ding als Objekt," Kunsthalle Nürnberg, West Germany
1969   "Kunst der Sechziger Jahre," Sammlung Ludwig, Wallraf-Richartz Museum, Cologne, West Germany
         "Human Concern/Personal Torment: The Grotesque in American Art," Whitney Museum of American Art, New York, NY (circulated)
         "Pop Art Redefined," Hayward Gallery, London, England
         "Kompas 4: West Coast USA," Stedelijk van Abbemuseum, Eindhoven, The Netherlands
1968   "Late Fifties at the Ferus," Los Angeles County Museum of Art, CA
         "When Art Becomes Form," Kunsthalle Bern, Switerland
         "Dokumenta 4," Kassel, West Germany
         "Dada, Surrealism and Their Heritage," The Museum of Modern Art, New York, NY
         "Los Angeles 6," Vancouver Art Gallery, British Columbia, Canada
         "The Machine," The Museum of Modern Art, New York, NY
1967   "American Sculpture of the Sixties," Los Angeles County Museum of Art, CA (circulated: Philadelphia Museum of Art, PA)
         "Protest and Hope," New School Art Center, New York, NY
1966   "Annual Exhibition of Contemporary American Sculpture and Prints," Whitney Museum of American Art, New York, NY
         "68th American Exhibition of Painting and Sculpture," The Art Institute of Chicago, IL

WORKS IN THE EXHIBITION

"The Beanery" (two views), 1965 (plates 25 and 26)*
7' × 22' × 6,' mixed media
Stedelijk Museum, Amsterdam, The Netherlands
Photographed by Delmore E. Scott

"Gossip," 1963*
23" × 14" × 18," mixed media

EDWARD KIENHOLZ

PLATE 27   *AIR*, 1983

STATEMENT

In ancient Haniwa tomb sculptures the house was used as a metaphor for the body. There were windows for eyes and open doors and chimney flues for the spirits to move in and out. Additionally, the house has been used as a metaphor for our mental behavior, private and public, order and chaos, inside and outside. Shapes, materials and styles have changed; but, essentially, I think the use of it as an image has remained the same.

Ken Little, 1983

SELECTED BIOGRAPHY

Born in Canyon, Texas, 1947
Lives in Norman, Oklahoma

Selected Honors

1982 National Endowment for the Arts, Artists's Fellowship
1981 Purchase Award, "National Cone Box Show," Purdue University Art Galleries, West Lafayette, IN
1977 Western States Arts Foundation, Craftsman's Fellowship

Selected Solo Exhibitions

1983 Honolulu Academy of Art, HI (circulated: Yellowstone Art Center, Billings, MT; Gallery of Art, University of Montana, Missoula, MT; Alberta College of Art Gallery, Calgary, Alberta, Canada)
"Shattered Portraits and Unlikely Heroes," John Michael Kohler Arts Center, Sheboygan, WI
1983, Quay Gallery, San Francisco, CA
80
1979 Eastern Washington State University, Cheney, WA
1978 Northern Arizona University, Flagstaff, AZ
1977 Sun Valley Center for the Arts, ID
1976 Art Galleries, University of Wisconsin, Milwaukee, WI
1976, Gallery of Visual Arts, University of Montana, Missoula, MT
75

Selected Group Exhibitions

1983 "Winterworks," Oklahoma Art Center, Oklahoma City, OK
"Southern Fictions," invitational exhibition, Contemporary Art Museum, Houston, TX
"Benefit Auction," Yellowstone Art Center, Billings, MT
"Remains To Be Seen," John Michael Kohler Arts Center, Sheboygan, WI
"4th Texas Sculpture Symposium," Patrick Gallery, Austin, TX
"Constructions," San Francisco International Airport, CA
"Warashina/Little," ASA Gallery, University of New Mexico Student Union, Albuquerque, NM
"Clay in Mexico '83," Art Museum, University of New Mexico, Albuquerque, NM
"Clay: A Medium for Personal Iconography," Elements Gallery, New York, NY
"Hats Off!," The New Museum, New York, NY
"American Clay Artists: Philadelphia '83," Clay Studio, Philadelphia, PA
"Caprock too!," University of New Mexico, Albuquerque, NM (circulated: Meachum Auditorium, University of Oklahoma, Norman, OK)
"The Raw Edge: Ceramics of the '80s," Hillwood Gallery, C.W. Post College, New York, NY
"A Sense of Humor," Visual Arts Center of Alaska, Anchorage, AK
"Animal Invitational," Security Pacific Bank Building, Los Angeles, CA
"Fleming, Mariscol, Warashina, Little," Kansas City Art Institute, MO
1982 "Pets and Beasts," Transamerica Pyramid Building, San Francisco, CA
"Sculptors at U.C. Davis: Past and Present," Richard Nelson Gallery of Art, University of California, Davis, CA
"Sculpture, Sacramento," Alta Gallery, Sacramento, CA
"First Annual Wild West Show," Alberta College of Art Gallery, Calgary, Alberta, Canada
"Faculty Exhibition," Museum of Art, University of Oklhoma, Norman, OK

"The Lawndale Competition," University of Houston, Lawndale Annex, TX
"Group Exhibition," Municipal Art Gallery, Barnsdall Park, Los Angeles, CA
1981 "Paint on Clay," John Michael Kohler Arts Center, Sheboygan, WI
"Inside/Out: The Self Beyond Likeness," Newport Harbor Art Museum, Newport Beach, CA
"Animal Images," Renwick Gallery of the Smithsonian Institution, Washington, D.C.
"National Cone Box Show," Purdue University Art Galleries, West Lafayette, IN
"The Image of the House in Contemporary Art," University of Houston, Lawndale Annex, TX (cat.)
"Contemporary Ceramics, from J. Mannheimer Collection," Museum of Art, University of Iowa, Iowa City, IA
1979 "100 Years of American Ceramics," Everson Museum of Art of Syracuse and Onondaga County, NY
"Large-Scale Ceramic Sculpture," Richard Nelson Gallery of Art, University of California, Davis, CA
"Survey of Northwest Ceramics," Seattle Art Museum, WA
"Viewpoint: Ceramics 1979," Grossmont College Art Galleries, El Cajon, CA
"Clay Attitudes," The Queens Museum, Flushing, NY
1977 "The Makers: Fiber, Clay and Metal," Art Galleries, Georgia State University, Atlanta, GA
1976 "Clay—The Medium and the Method," Art Galleries, University of California, Santa Barbara, CA
"1976 Ceramic Conjunction," Long Beach Museum of Art, CA
"Montana Sculptors," Yellowstone Art Center, Billings, MT
1975 "National Ceramic Invitational," Art Galleries, University of Colorado, Boulder, CO
1974 "Clay Image," California State University, Los Angeles, CA
1973 "Image–Idea," Evanston Art Center, IL

WORKS IN THE EXHIBITION

"Air," 1983 (plate 27)**
65" × 36" × 37," leather, paint and mixed media
Lent by the artist
Photographed by A. Strout

KEN LITTLE

PLATE 28   *BEEHIVE*, 1979

STATEMENT

A house is a living space where elemental functions are carried out. The elemental functions of sleeping, eating, eliminating and hygenic needs, sexual and private activities and social or group activities regulate the allocation of space in our houses. "Rooms" for these different activities are common to all structures, the discrepancies in size, situation and elaborateness reflecting priorities of the inhabitant.

That is the fascination of architecture, houses or public buildings. In understanding that the outer reflects the inner, we have found a key to understanding some pre-occupations of cultures and individuals. From the New York City street bum who has a totally public sense of space (a cardboard box or just a coat for a house that marks hs private boundaries) to the palatial extravagances of kings and millionaires, the built exteriors are clues to the inner psyche.

Believing this, I become greatly concerned looking at the architecture surrounding us. The psyche revealed is a very lopsided, very forbidding one. My architecturally related sculptures are a response to this. Their original referent was a simple, compact, symmetrical farmhouse, analogous to a head with eyes and mouth—similar also in that both house and head are central organizers and sieves through which the outer world is perceived.

I would like architecture and our total environment to once again refer to the body, be an extension and expansion of the body, to be an organic system that has a flow and interconnectedness that brings a sense of vitality that undeniably a majority of our cities does not have.

Recent developments in technology have led to the appearance of tent-like stretched-skin structures, often mammoth, which present the possibility of once more seeing in the built landscape organically referential structures which not only serve a function, but please the eye.

Charmaine Locke, 1983

SELECTED BIOGRAPHY

Born in Waltham, Massachusetts, 1950
Lives in Splendora, Texas

Selected Group Exhibitions

1983 "Artists of the Southwest," The Sculpture Center, New York, NY
"Connemara Outdoor Sculpture Exhibition," Connemara, Dallas, TX
"Invitational '83," Longview Museum and Art Center, NY Longview, NY
1982 "Group Show," Newell Gallery, Houston, TX
"The Houston Festival," First International Bank Plaza, Houston, TX
1981 "The Image of the House in Contemporary Art," University of Houston, Lawndale Annex, TX (cat.)
"Sumfest '81," University of Houston, Lawndale Annex, TX
"Collection '81–The Road Show," 2 Houston Center, TX
1980 "Couples," Fendrick Gallery, Washington, D.C.
"Houston in Dallas," 500 Exposition Gallery, Dallas, TX
"National Sculpture Exhibition," Maryland Institute, College of Art, Baltimore, MD
"Two from Texas," Galerie Simonne Stern, New Orleans, LA
"Charmaine Locke and James Surls," Stephen F. Austin College, Nacogdoches, TX
"Temples," Max Hutchinson Gallery, Houston, TX

"18 Texans," Corpus Christi State University, TX
"Fire," Contemporary Arts Museum, Houston, TX
"13th Annual National Drawing and Small Sculpture Show," Del Mar College, Corpus Christi, TX, 1979 Award Winner
"A Closer Look," Contemporary Arts Museum, Houston, TX
"Miniature Show," University of Houston, Lawndale Annex, TX
1978 "The Bag Show," Delta Gallery, Houston, TX
"The Tree Show," D.W. Co-op Gallery, Dallas, TX
1977 "Group Show," Max Hutchinson Gallery, Houston, TX

WORKS IN THE EXHIBITION

"Calm at the Center," 1982*
17' x 16' x 16'; exterior: pine, roofing and plexiglass; interior: mixed media environment
Site: First International Bank Plaza, Houston, TX

"Beehive," 1979 (plate 28)
20" x 15" x 15," earth, glue and mahogany
Lent by the artist
Photographed by Charmaine Locke

61

CHARMAINE LOCKE

PLATE 29   *VALERIAN OVERTURE*, 1983

62

STATEMENT

It is more through the process of stacking and layering that I came to see my work as architectonic. There is a floor plan made up of lath lines describing simple geometries. The structure evolves vertically and forms walls which make enclosures; there are openings which become entrances.

The lath holds itself together by its own weight. The structure stands on its terms and describes its own visual logic—from without and within. It stands for as long as intended.

Completion is never achieved in spite of all conclusions.

Edward Mayer, 1983

SELECTED BIOGRAPHY

Born in Union, New Jersey, 1942
Lives in Athens, Ohio

Selected Honors

1981 Ohio Arts Council Fellowship
1979 National Endowment for the Arts, Artist's Fellowship
Ohio Arts Council Fellowship
P.S. 1 Studio Residency Grant, The Institute for Art and Urban Resources, Long Island City, NY
1978 National Endowment for the Arts, Artist's Fellowship
Ohio Arts Council Fellowship

Selected Solo Exhibitions

1983 1708 East Main, Richmond, VA
1982 Hartford Art School, University of Hartford, CT
Central Park Zoo, New York, NY
Herron Gallery, Herron School of Art, Indianapolis, IN
Columbus Museum of Art, OH
Dobrick Gallery, Chicago, IL
1981 Clemson University, SC
Rose Art Museum, Brandeis University, Waltham, MA
University of Missouri, Kansas City, MO
Southeastern Center for Contemporary Art, Winston-Salem, NC
1980 Nassau County Museum of Fine Arts, Roslyn, NY
Zabriskie Gallery, New York, NY
1978 Kunsthalle, Darmstadt, West Germany
Brown University, Providence, RI
O.K. Harris Gallery, New York, NY

Selected Group Exhibitions

1983 "5 Ohio Artists," Akron Art Museum, OH
"Installation for 4th Texas Sculpture Symposium," Archer M. Huntington Art Gallery, Austin, TX
1983- "New Directions: Contemporary Art from the Commodities Cor-
82 poration Collection," Museum of Art, Fort Lauderdale, FL (circulated: Oklahoma Museum of Art, Oklahoma City, OK; The Santa Barbara Museum of Art, CA; Grand Rapids Art Museum, MI; Madison Art Center, Inc., WI; Montgomery Museum of Fine Arts, AL)
1982 "Prints by Contemporary Sculptors," Yale University Art Gallery, New Haven, CT
"Mile of Sculpture: Art EXPO," Chicago Sculpture Society, Navy Pier, Chicago, IL
"Inside/Out: 3 Environmental Sculpturs," Dairy Barn, Athens, OH
"Wood into the '80s," Turman Gallery, Indiana State University, Terre Haute, IN
1980 "Architectural Sculpture," Los Angeles Institute of Contemporary Art, CA (cat.)
"Stacking, Rigging and Binding," Washington Project for the Arts, Washington, D.C.
"Five Ohio Sculptors," Contemporary Arts Center, Cincinnati, OH
"Stacked, Packed and Hung," N.A.M.E. Gallery, Chicago, IL
"Architectural Sculpture," Hunter College, New York, NY
1978 "New Talent," Zabriskie Gallery, New York, NY

WORKS IN THE EXHIBITION

"Rite Site" (outdoor installation), 1983
9' x 15' x 30,' stacked wood lath
Site: California State University, Fullerton, CA

"Valerian Overture," 1983 (plate 29, cat. only)
11' x 16' x 35 ' (approx.), stacked wood
Site: 1708 East Main, Richmond, VA
Photographed by Edward Mayer

"P.S. 1-1," 1979*
16' x 16' x 10,' stacked wood

"P.S. 1-4," 1979*
8' x 18' x 20,' stacked wood

EDWARD MAYER

PLATE 30   *MONUMENT TO THE LIGHT AT THE END OF THE TUNNEL, 1982*

64

STATEMENT

Most of us operate within a limited model of reality, and look for what confirms rather than challenges our pre-conceptions.

I'd like to keep my model open and in progress. In the big picture, I'm interested by incongruity and harmony—the resolution of opposition by rhythmic balance. With tangents and time-outs here and there, my approach is to combine painting with sculpture, the implied with the actual. This seems almost a physical exemplification of opposition and resolution. Of course combining painting and sculpture creates a conundrum, and in dealing with this a sense of irony is useful.

My working method is traditional, rather conservative, grounded in drawing and the study of traditional painting and woodworking. My images and ideas come from many sources: nineteenth-century engineering, Japanese prints and proportion, classical architecture, late Gothic altar-pieces, the art of our century.

I try to produce work that is intriguing and accessible, but perhaps not explicable. I hope to capture some of the small, inexpressible mystery in each day. There is much to be felt and recorded of the unseen trace of our lives in structures and rooms we build and inhabit. My most successful work evolves beyond my own understanding of it, seeming to take on a life of its own. It acts as a beacon in the gap between intention and accomplishment.

Stephan McKeown, 1983

SELECTED BIOGRAPHY

Born in Pasadena, California, 1947
Lives in New York, New York

Selected Solo Exhibitions

1983 Robert Freidus Gallery, New York, NY
1982 Neil G. Ovsey Gallery, Los Angeles, CA
Mattingly-Baker Gallery, Dallas, TX
1981 Robert Freidus Gallery, New York, NY
Neil G. Ovsey Gallery, Los Angeles, CA
1980 State University of New York, College at Brockport, NY
Robert Freidus Gallery, New York, NY
1979 "Constructions," Robert Hull Fleming Museum, University of Vermont, Burlington, VT
1977 "Recent Drawings," Colburn Gallery, University of Vermont, Burlington, VT
1976 St. Michael's College, Winooski, VT

Selected Group Exhibitions

1983 Neil G. Ovsey Gallery, Los Angeles, CA
1983- "Wood & Fiber Invitational," Columbia Museum, SC
82
"Wall Reliefs," Rotunda Gallery, Brooklyn, NY
1982 "Summer Group Show," Neil G. Ovsey Gallery, Los Angeles, CA
1981 "Wallworks," University of Southern California, Los Angeles, CA
"Some Painters for Example," Security Pacific Bank, Los Angeles, CA
Neil G. Ovsey Gallery, Los Angeles, CA
"Some Recent Sculpture," Tyler School of Art, Philadelphia, PA
1980- "Art for the Vice President's House from Northeast Museums,"
79 Washington, D.C.
1978 "Faculty Exhibition," Robert Hull Fleming Museum, University of Vermont, Burlington, VT
1977 "New Talent," Allan Stone Gallery, New York, NY
1976 "Vermont, 1976," Bundy Gallery, Waitsfield, VT

Selected Public Collections
The Museum of Modern Art (Graphics Department), New York, NY

National Gallery of Australia, Canberra, Australia
Roland Gibson Foundation, State University of New York, College at Potsdam, NY
Robert Hull Fleming Museum, University of Vermont, Burlington, VT
Dartmouth College, Hanover, NH

WORKS IN THE EXHIBITION

"Monument to the Light at the End of the Tunnel," 1982 (plate 30)**
51" × 48½" × 18½," polychromed wood and panel
Courtesy of Neil G. Ovsey Gallery, Los Angeles, CA
Photograph courtesy of Neil G. Ovsey Gallery, Los Angeles, CA

STEPHAN McKEOWN

PLATE 31   *MIKE'S POOL HALL*, 1977

STATEMENT

The corner of a dilapidated hotel standing in isolation on a pedestal; a streamline moderne diner hovering in the air over a barren expanse strewn with bones; a power plant nestling in a rocky, burned-out landscape; a weathered door approached by ruined stairs and hanging on an empty wall; a partially mummified skeleton reclining on a battered chaise in the Mojave Desert—fantastic images of disaster and decay form a continuous thread in his work.

The sham ruin is associated with the larger concept of "the picturesque." As the ordered manipulation of natural and artificial elements to create a physical structure that simulates a picture, the picturesque acts as both a decorative scene and as a catalyst for meditation.

From Christopher Knight in *Arts and Architecture*, *Fall 1981, p. 22.*

SELECTED BIOGRAPHY

Born in Los Angeles, California, 1946
Lives in Santa Monica, California

Selected Honors

1978   New Talent Purchase Award, Contemporary Arts Council, Los Angeles County Museum of Art, CA
National Endowment for the Arts, Artist's Fellowship

Selected Solo Exhibitions

1982   Asher/Faure Gallery, Los Angeles, CA
Macquarie Galleries, Sydney, Australia
1981   "The Floating Diner" (installation), Pittsburgh Center for the Arts, PA
1980   Asher/Faure Gallery, Los Angeles, CA
Macquarie Galleries, Sydney, Australia
"Project 29: Michael McMillen," Art Gallery of New South Wales, Sydney, Australia
1978   "Inner City," Whitney Museum of American Art, New York, NY
"Ray Cathode's Garden" (installation), Cerro Coso College, Ridgecrest, CA
1977   "Inner City" (installation), Los Angeles County Museum of Art, CA
1973   "The Traveling Mystery Museum," Venice, CA
1969   Bay Cities Jewish Community Center, Santa Monica, CA
"Transient Images: A Kinetic Environment," San Fernando Valley State College, San Fernando, CA

Selected Group Exhibitions

1983   "Young Talent Awards: 1963-1983," Los Angeles County Museum of Art, CA (cat.)
"New Perspectives in American Art: 1983 Exxon National Exhibition," The Solomon R. Guggenheim Museum, New York, NY
"The 38th Corcoran Biennial Exhibition of American Painting," Corcoran Gallery of Art, Washington, D.C. (cat.)
1982   "Art and Survival," Traction Gallery, Los Angeles, CA
"The Sydney Harbour Bridge," Art Gallery of New South Wales, Sydney, Australia
"5 From LA," Mandeville Art Gallery, University of California, San Diego, La Jolla, CA
1981   "Locations," California State College, San Bernardino, CA
"Art in Los Angeles—The Museum as Site: Sixteen Projects," Los Angeles County Museum of Art, CA (cat.)
"Humor in Art," Los Angeles Institute of Contemporary Art, CA
1980   "Architectural Sculpture," Fine Arts Gallery, Mount St. Mary's College, Los Angeles, CA (organized by Los Angeles Institute of Contemporary Art, CA) (cat.)
"Tableau—An American Selection," Middendorf/Lane Gallery, Washington, D.C.
"In a Major and Minor Scale," Municipal Art Gallery, Barnsdall Park, Los Angeles, CA
"Sculpture in California 1975–80," San Diego Art Museum, CA
"Tableau," Los Angeles Institute of Contemporary Art, CA

1979   "Eight Artists: The Elusive Image," Walker Art Center, Minneapolis, MN
"The Artist as Social Critic—1979," Municipal Art Gallery, Barnsdall Park, Los Angeles, CA
"Los Angeles in the Seventies," Joslyn Art Museum, Omaha, NB
1978   "Artists' Books—Bookworks," Australia (circulated)
"Other Things that Artists Make," Municipal Art Gallery, Barnsdall Park, Los Angeles, CA
"Eccentric Los Angeles Art," ARCO Center for Visual Art, Los Angeles, CA
"A Proposal for a Children's Museum," Baxter Art Gallery, California Institute of Technology, Pasadena, CA
1978   "The Subject is the Object," Baum-Silverman Gallery, Los Angeles, CA
"Art Words and Bookworks," Los Angeles Institute of Conporary Art, CA
1977   "Los Angeles in the Seventies," Fort Worth Art Museum, TX
"Miniature," California State University, Los Angeles, CA
"We All Were Here," California State University, Northridge, CA
1976   "Biennale of Sydney—November, 1976," Australia
"Summer Show," SPACE Gallery, Los Angeles, CA
"Imagination," Los Angeles Institute of Contemporary Art, CA
1975   "Sounds: Audio-Visual Environments by Four LA Artists," Newport Harbor Art Museum, Newport Beach, CA
"Eight Artists from Los Angeles," San Francisco Art Institute, CA
"Crucifixes," Betty Gold Gallery, Los Angeles, CA
1974   "First Annual California Sculpture Exhibition," California State University, Northridge, CA
1972   "Fifth California Small Images Exhibition," California State University, Los Angeles, CA

WORKS IN THE EXHIBITION

"Mike's Pool Hall," 1977 (plate 31)
11" × 21" × 12," mixed media
Courtesy of Asher/Faure Gallery, Los Angeles, CA
Photographed by Mark Schwartz

"Caledonia," 1980*
49" × 19' × 17½," mixed media

MICHAEL McMILLEN

PLATE 32   *FALSEWORK: CAGED LADDER,* 1980

68

STATEMENT

There was a "Twilight Zone" story about a man who spent a great deal of time trying to figure out how he could walk through a brick wall. With all of his resources summoned, he stepped forward and actually walked into the wall—but there was a problem: it was not possible for him to come out on the other side. He remained encased in that brick wall.

At times, as an artist interested in doing "public art," working in the context of the built environment, I feel that I share something of the predicament of this character. As much interest as I may have, it is very difficult for an artist to find an access route in this culture to public situations.

Art must be experienced directly. The public today lives in a world animated by electronic communications (which perhaps dampens or discourages "direct experience"). Meanwhile, the image of art as often conveyed through the media remains historical. It is something to be labeled and put away.

From Mary Miss, "Toward a Redefinition of Public Sculpture," *Metropolis: Locus of Contemporary Myth* (U.S./Japan Symposium on Urban Life and Culture, October 1–4, 1982), pp. 7, 8.

SELECTED BIOGRAPHY

Born in New York, New York, 1944
Lives in New York, New York

Selected Honors

1982 Creative Arts Award, Brandeis University, Waltham, MA
1976 New York State Council on the Arts, Creative Artists Public Service Grant
1975 National Endowment for the Arts, Artist's Fellowship
1974 National Endowment for the Arts, Artist's Fellowship
Project Grant, Mott Community College, Flint, MI
1973 New York State Council on the Arts, Creative Artists Public Service Grant

Selected Solo Exhibitions

1982 "Mary Miss," Laumeier Sculpture Park, St. Louis, MO
1981 "Mary Miss," Brown University and University of Rhode Island, Kingston, RI
"Directions '81," Museum of Art, Rhode Island School of Design, Providence, RI
1980 "Falsework," Max Protetch Gallery, New York, NY
"Mirror Way," Fogg Art Museum, Harvard University, Cambridge, MA (cat.)
1979 "Screened Court," Minneapolis College of Art and Design, MN
1978 "Perimeters/Pavilions/Decoys," Nassau County Museum of Fine Arts, Roslyn, NY (cat.)
1976 "Projects," The Museum of Modern Art, New York, NY
1975 Salvatore Ala Gallery, Milan, Italy
Rosa Esman Gallery, New York, NY
1972, 55 Mercer Gallery, new York, NY
71

Selected Site Works

1981 "Field Rotation," Governors State University, Park Forest South, IL
1979 "Staged Gates," Dayton, OH
"Veiled Landscape," XIII Winter Olympic Games, Lake Placid, NY
1976 "Blind Set," ArtPark, Lewiston, NY
1974 "Sunken Pool," Greenwich, CT
1973 "Untitled," Allen Memorial Art Museum, Oberlin College, OH (permanently installed 1975)
"Untitled" (landfill), Battery Park City, New York, NY

1969 "V's in the Field," Liberty Corner, NY
"Ropes/Shores," Wards Island, NJ
1968 "Stakes and Ropes," Colorado Springs, CO
"Window in Hill," Colorado Springs, CO

Selected Group Exhibitions

1982 "Utopia and City," Neuer Berliner Kunstverein, West Berlin, West Germany
1981 "Artists' Gardens and Parks," Hayden Gallery, Massachusetts Institute of Technology, Cambridge, MA (circulated: Museum of Contemporary Art, Chicago, IL)
"The Whitney Biennial Exhibition of Painting and Sculpture," Whitney Museum of American Art, New York, NY (cat.)
"The Image of the House in Contemporary Art," University of Houston, Lawndale Annex, TX (cat.)
1980 "Drawings: The Pluralist Decade," 39th Venice Biennale, United States Pavilion, Italy (circulated: Institute of Contemporary Art, University of Pennsylvania, Philadelphia, PA; Museum of Contemporary Art, Chicago, IL) (cat.)
"Architectural Sculpture," Fine Arts Gallery, Mount St. Mary's College, Los Angeles, CA (organized by Los Angeles Institute of Contemporary Art, CA) (cat.)
"A Sense of Place," Hampshire College, Amherst, MA
1979 "Art and Architecture, Space and Structure," Protech-McIntosh Gallery, Washington, D.C.
1978 "Architectural Analogues," Whitney Museum Downtown Branch, New York, NY (cat.)
1977 "Nine Artists: The Theodoran Awards," The Solomon R. Guggenheim Museum, New York, NY
"Women in Architecture," The Brooklyn Museum, NY
"Drawings for Outdoor Sculpture, 1946-1977," John Weber Gallery, New York, NY
"Site Sculpture," Zabriskie Gallery, New York, NY
1976 "Rooms," P.S. 1, The Institute for Art and Urban Resources, Long Island City, NY
"New York: Downtown Soho," Akademie der Kunst, West Berlin, West Germany
"Drawing/Transparency," Cannaviello Studio d'Arte, Piazza de Massimi, Rome, Italy
1974 "Interventions in Landscape: Projects/Documentation/Film/Video," Hayden Gallery, Massachusetts Institute of Technology, Cambridge, MA
1973 "The Whitney Biennial Exhibition of Painting and Sculpture," Whitney Museum of American Art, New York, NY
1972 "GEDOK American Women Artists," Kunsthaus, Hamburg, West Germany
1971 "26 Contemporary Women Artists," Aldrich Museum of Contemporary Art, Ridgefield, CT

WORKS IN THE EXHIBITION

"Falsework: Caged Ladder," 1980 (plate 32)
9' × 4' × 7'6," wood, wire mesh and steel
Lent by the artist
Photographed by Mary Miss

"Field Rotation," 1981*
56' square × 7' deep on four and one-half acres; steel, wood and earth
Site: Governors State University, Forest Park South, IL

"Veiled Landscape" (two detail views), 1979*
10' × 10' × 15'; 400' from first structure to last; steel and wood
Site: XIII Winter Olympic Games, Lake Placid, NY

"Staged Gates," 1979*
12' × 50' × 120,' wood
Site: Dayton, OH

"Perimeters/Pavilions/Decoys" (detail view), 1978*
16' × 16' opening on four acres; earth and wood
Site: Nassau County Museum of Fine Arts, Roslyn, NY

MARY MISS

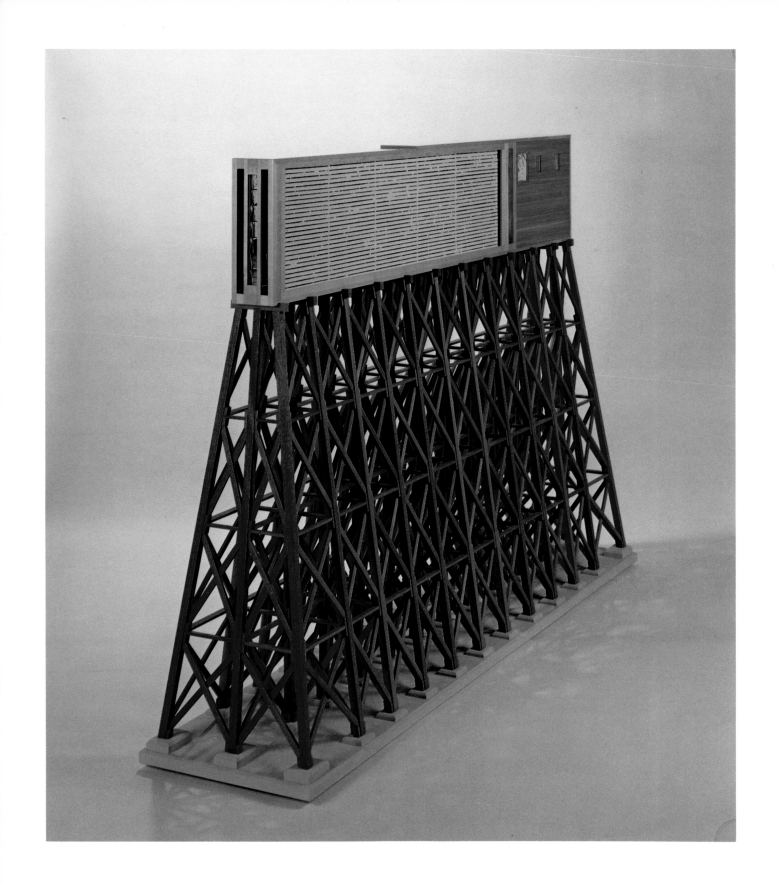

PLATE 33   *EL REPOSO ABANDONADO, 1982–83*

70

STATEMENT

I'm trying to make things as inspiring and open for raw experience as daily living . . . to paint or construct a potentially novel, thought provoking environment/adventure for myself and the viewer.

From eighteen years at the farm in Michigan, to a secluded "jungle house" in Miami (named EL REPOSO by a previous occupant) to a multi-tenant warehouse in Costa Mesa . . . the frequencies have all changed. Additions are being built onto my perception of "Home." The work is my estate.

Also, still in my youth—and occasionally back at the farm—I do some things "for the hell of it." That's the logic of artistic invention, and the spirit of experiment. Called many things by many people, there's a bit of "for the hell of it" in all fine works of art. It's that aspect easiest to see or to not see, and what we come here to look for.

Douglas R. Moran, 1983

SELECTED BIOGRAPHY

Born in Allegan, Michigan, 1949
Lives in Costa Mesa, California

Selected Solo Exhibitions

1983 "Surroundings," TLK Gallery, Costa Mesa, CA
1982 "Recent Drawings," Gloria Luria Gallery, Miami, FL
1981 "Doug Moran, Wallscapes 1976–1981," University of Southern California, Los Angeles, CA (cat.)
"Wallscapes: Doug Moran," Jack Rasmussen Gallery, Washington, D.C.
1980 "Doug Moran: Wallscape Painting," Gloria Luria Gallery, Miami, FL
1975 "Doug Moran: Works on Paper," Corcoran-Greenberg Gallery, Coral Gables, FL

Site Works

1982- "Adjacent Facades," Coronado Business Park, Anaheim, CA
80
1979 "Industrial Facade," Standard Concrete Materials building, Santa Ana, CA
1978 "Southeast Wallscape/Wesgate," Federal Building and U.S. Courthouse, Fort Lauderdale, FL
1975 "Miami Flyer," Miami-Dade Community College, Miami, FL

Selected Group Exhibitions

1982 "Visiting Artist," Claremont Graduate College, CA
Gensler and Associates, Architects, Irvine, CA
"Gallery Artists," Koplin Gallery, Los Angeles, CA
1981 Norton Gallery and School of Art, West Palm Beach, FL
1980 "Drawings of Southern California," University of Hartford, West Hartford, CT
1979 "Our Own Artists: Art in Orange County," Newport Harbor Art Museum, Newport Beach, CA (cat.)
"Paintings," Janus Gallery, Venice, CA
"Drawings," Jack Rasmussen Gallery, Washington, D.C.
1978 Dade County Public Library, Miami, Miami Lakes, Cutler Ridge, FL
1977 "Permanent Collection," Museum of Art, Fort Lauderdale, FL
1976 Metropolitan Museum and Art Center, Miami, FL
Corcoran-Greenberg Gallery, Coral Gables, FL
The Society of Four Arts, Palm Beach, FL
Museum of Art, Fort Lauderdale, FL
1975 Art and Cultural Center of Hollywood, FL
Museum of Art, Fort Lauderdale, FL
1974 The Society of Four Arts, Palm Beach, FL
Metropolitan Museum and Art Center, Miami, FL
Miami-Dade Community College, Miami, FL

Selected Public Collections

National Collection of Fine Arts, Smithsonian Institution, Washington, D.C.
Horowitz Brothers Trust, Santa Ana, CA
Atlantic Richfield Company, Los Angeles, CA
Dade County Public Libraries, Miami, FL
Metropolitan Museum and Art Center, Coral Gables, FL
Museum of Art, Fort Lauderdale, FL
Norton Gallery and School of Art, West Palm Beach, FL
Southeast Banking Corporation, Miami, FL
Joseph Hirshhorn, Greenwich, CT
Bank of Beverly Hills, Los Angeles, CA
Citicorp Bank, New York, NY

WORKS IN THE EXHIBITION

"El Reposo Abandonado," 1982–83 (plate 33)
57" x 19" x 83½," wood, glass, stone, lacquer and encaustic
Lent by the artist
Photographed by Jerry Newton

"Dairy Suite I," 1982*
24" x 48" x 3," wood, glass, acrylic and wire

DOUGLAS MORAN

PLATE 34   *HOLD OUT/HOLDING ON*, 1982

72

STATEMENT

The *Real Estate* series began with the purchase of my first home. I was brought up believing that the largest financial (and a great emotional) investment a family will make is the purchase of a house. At the time, I found myself bidding against two realtors for what was to be my home. They wanted to paint it and resell it strictly for investment. The reduction of home to object led me to reduce the image to a very small scale. On a formal level, the single point perspective is an attempt to draw the viewer into the piece. The houses are made from memory, rather than photographs, in an attempt to appear familiar to the viewer by tapping into his or her memory. I wanted these very familiar little houses so the viewer would almost be put into them and say, "I know this house," and then stand back and see that they've been turned into these very tiny objects of speculation. They stand isolated, alone, and yet, hopefully, their compact image commands an area—emotionally and formally greater than their physical size.

Gifford Chandler Myers, 1983

SELECTED BIOGRAPHY

Born in Palo Alto, California, 1948
Lives in Altadena, California

Selected Honors
1979 National Endowment for the Arts, Artist's Fellowship
1976 First Award, "All California Art Exhibition," San Bernardino, CA
First Award, "California State Fair Art Show," Sacramento, CA
1974 First Award, "Hayward Festival of Art," CA
Purchase Award, "All California Ceramic Annual," California State University, San Mateo, CA
1972 First Award, "Hayward Festival of Art," CA
Purchase Award, "All California Ceramic Annual," California State University, San Mateo, CA

Selected Solo Exhibitions
1982 Municipal Art Gallery, Barnsdall Park, Los Angeles, CA
McIntosh/Drysdale Gallery, Washington, D.C.
1981 Janus Gallery, Los Angeles, CA
Orange County Center for Contemporary Art, Santa Ana, CA
1976 Riverside Art Museum, CA
1975 University of California, Irvine, CA

Selected Group Exhibitions
1983 "Constructions," San Francisco International Airport, CA
"Ceramic Echoes," Kansas City Art Museum, MO
1982 "Aspects of Sculpture," John Berggruen Gallery, San Francisco, CA
"Made in L.A.," Federal Reserve Board, Washington, D.C.
"Microcosms," Siegel Contemporary Art, Inc., New York, NY
"Microcosms," Contemporary Arts Forum, Santa Barbara, CA
"Pacific Currents," San Jose Museum of Art, CA
"The Kanazawa Exhibition," Kanazawa, Japan
"Houses," The Sculpture Center, New York, NY
"Collectors Choice," Baltimore Museum of Art, MD
Fedral Reserve Board, Washington, D.C.
Siegel Contemporary Art, Inc., New York, NY
1981 "California: The State of Landscape, 1872–1981," Newport Harbor Art Museum, Newport Beach, CA (cat.)
"Humor in Art," Los Angeles Institute of Contemporary Art, CA
"New West '82," Suzanne Brown Gallery, Scottsdale, AZ
Molly Barnes Gallery, Los Angeles, CA
"Locations," California State University, San Bernardino, CA
"Anti-Static," California Institute of Technology, Pasadena, CA
1980 "Ceramic National," Otis-Parsons, Los Angeles, CA, and New York, NY
1979 Asher/Faure Gallery, Los Angeles, CA
Anhalt/Barnes Gallery, Los Angeles, CA

1979, Municipal Art Gallery, Barnsdall Park, Los Angeles, CA
78
1978 "West Coast Clay Spectrum," Security Pacific Bank Headquarters, Los Angeles, CA
"Miniatures," California State University, Los Angeles, CA
"Group Show," Mizuno Gallery, Los Angeles, CA
1977 "Words," Whitney Museum Downtown Branch, New York, NY
"Illusionistic Realism in Contemporary Ceramic Sculpture," Laguna Beach Museum of Art, CA
"Atmospheres," Bank of America Headquarters, San Francisco, CA
"Ceramic Conjunction VII," Long Beach Museum of Art, CA
"Four L.A. Surrealists," Jacqueline Anhalt Gallery, Los Angeles, CA
Mano Gallery, Chicago, IL
1976 California State University, San Bernardino, CA
Jacqueline Anhalt Gallery, Los Angeles, CA
Quay Ceramics Gallery, San Francisco, CA
"All California Sculpture and Painting," Laguna Beach Museum of Art, CA
Fendrick Gallery, Washington, D.C.
San Francisco Museum of Art, Sales and Rentals Gallery, CA
Newport Harbor Art Museum, Sales and Rentals Gallery, Newport Beach, CA
1975 "Ceramic Conjunction V," Brand Library Art Center, Glendale, CA
"Irvine, The Last Decade," La Jolla Museum of Contemporary Art, CA
1974 "The Cup Show II," David Stuart Gallery, Los Angeles, CA
1972 "The Cup Show," David Stuart Gallery, Los Angeles, CA
1971 "The Metal Experience," Oakland Art Museum, CA

WORKS IN THE EXHIBITION

"Hold Out/Holding On," 1982 (plate 34)**
12" × 6½" × 2¾," acrylic and glaze on ceramic
Lent by Richard and Rosemary Bergen
Photographed by Mark Schwartz

GIFFORD MYERS

PLATE 35   *IT'S ALL DONE WITH COMPUTERS*, 1983

74

STATEMENT

To make a work of art as simple as the concept of zero.
—Orr

Plato was on the right track when he said, "The weakness of art is that artists are imitating an imitation." —Orr
The *commode* is the dividing line between art and architecture. —Orr
In the field of architecture and art, *Imhotep* said it all.
—Orr
The future of art depends on artists not copying art but finding it. —Orr
I use silence the way a painter uses color. —Orr
Why is space active and object passive? —Orr
The artist of the future will address states of mind. —Orr
Does transient afternoon light on the wall look better than art? —Orr
My fondest enemy is the way one idea terrorizes another.
—Orr

Eric Orr, 1983

The meeting ground of art and architecture is collage: e.g., window, light fixture, sink, furniture, walls, etc.
—Fisher
Fragments of the profane ground new work and, conversely, new insertions change normal situations. —Fisher

Frederick Fisher, 1983

SELECTED BIOGRAPHY
Born in Covington, Kentucky, 1939
Lives in Los Angeles, California

Selected Solo Exhibitions
1982 Taylor Gallery, Taos, NM
1982, Neil G. Ovsey Gallery, Los Angeles, CA
81
1980 "Silence and the Ion Wind," Los Angeles County Museum of Art, CA
"Infinite Gold Void," Los Angeles Institute of Contemporary Art, CA
1979 "Chemical Light," Janus Gallery, Los Angeles, CA
1978 "Drawings for the Gold Room," Cirrus Gallery, Los Angeles, CA
"Seasons of the Fountain," Delahunty Gallery, Dallas, TX
1976 "Sunrise," Cirrus Gallery, Los Angeles, CA
1975 Salvatore Ala Gallery, Milano, Italy
1974 Cirrus Gallery, Los Angeles, CA
1973 University of California, Irvine, CA
1968 Eugenia Butler Gallery, Los Angeles, CA

Selected Group Exhibitions
1983 Neil G. Ovsey Gallery, Los Angeles, CA
"Fire and Water," Neil G. Ovsey Gallery, Los Angeles, CA
1982 "Dokumenta 7," Kassel, West Germany
"Art as Alchemy," California State University, Dominguez Hills, CA
1981 "Museum as Site,"Los Angeles County Museum of Art, CA
"Light and Space," Lonny Gans & Associates, Venice, CA
1980 "Fire as Prime Matter," Libra Gallery, Claremont, CA
"Lead/Gold Reliefs" and "Seasons of the Fountain," Neil G. Ovsey Gallery, Sherman Oaks, CA
"New Works," Cirrus Gallery, Los Angeles, CA
1979 "California," University of Hartford, CT
"Works on Glass," Minneapolis Art Center, MN
1977 "L.A. of the 70s," Fort Worth Art Museum, TX
1975 "Transparency Exhibition," Long Beach Museum of Art, CA
Newport Harbor Art Museum, Newport Beach, CA

1974 "Three to One," Junior Arts Center, Barnsdall Park, Los Angeles, CA
1974-73 "Stone Serpent," Municipal Art Gallery, Barnsdall Park, Los Angeles, CA
1973-71 "Infinity Space," University of California, Irvine, CA
1971 "Glass Shadow," Giza, Egypt
1971-70 "Sound Tunnel," Municipal Art Gallery, Barnsdall Park, Los Angeles, CA (circulated: University of Southern California, Los Angeles, CA)
1970 "Sound in Shape of Pear," Museum of Contemporary Crafts, New York, NY
1969 "357 Magnum," Düsseldorf, West Germany
"Search Light Sky Shapes," California Institute of Technology, Pasadena, CA
"Wall Shadow," Eugenia Butler Gallery, Los Angeles, CA
"Wall Shadow," California State University, Los Angeles, CA
"Volumetric Sound," San Francisco Art Institute, CA
"The Electric Show," University of California, Los Angeles, CA
1968 "Dry Ice," University of California, San Diego, CA
"Sky Lights," Century City, Los Angeles, CA
"Room Company #2," Century City, Los Angeles, CA
"Tracer Bullets," Figueroa Street, Los Angeles, CA
"Fresh Air," Pershing Square, Los Angeles, CA
"1,000 to 1," Griffith Park, Los Angeles, CA
1967 "Fresh Air Space," Municipal Art Gallery, Barnsdall Park, Los Angeles, CA
"Vandenburg Letters," sky over Los Angeles, CA
1966 "Room Company #1," Rolf Nelson Gallery, Los Angeles, CA

WORKS IN THE EXHIBITION

"It's All Done with Computers" (with Frederick Fisher and David Martin), 1983 (plate 35)
27½" × 23½," gold leaf and blood
Courtesy of Neil G. Ovsey Gallery, Los Angeles, CA
Photographed by Mark Schwartz

"Blind Windows" (diptych), 1981*
24" × 17" each panel; lead and gold leaf

ERIC ORR

PLATE 36   *TWO HUNDRED YEARS OF ARCHITECTURE: A BICENTENNIAL SALUTE TO LOS ANGELES 1781–1981*, 1980

STATEMENT

From May 23 to June 23, 1981, I commemorated the Los Angeles Bicentennial with a site-specific architectural installation entitled, *Two Hundred Years of Architecture: A Bicentennial Salute to Los Angeles 1781–1981.* I described it as "an end to westward expansion," dedicated to Horace Greeley.

The site of the installation was a prime acre of oceanfront realty between Paradise Cove and Point Dume on the Malibu cliffs. Occupying the undeveloped lot were 794 identical blue houses, each 8 × 11 × 8 inches in size, with pine clapboard siding and peaked metal roofs. Uniform rows of houses arranged in a 65 × 260-foot grid ran to the edge of the cliff, with a view of the Malibu beach 80 feet below. The sprawling Los Angeles skyline could be seen on the eastern horizon.

Individual houses were offered for sale, subject to contract and priced according to their proximity to the ocean, through Asher/Faure in Los Angeles. The Los Angeles Institute of Contemporary Art (LAICA), in cooperation with Asher/Faure, sponsored a contemporaneous indoor exhibition.

This exhibition at Express Network, one year later, showed the northeast portion of the Malibu installation.

Stephen Pearson, 1983

SELECTED BIOGRAPHY

Born in Santa Monica, California, 1946
Lives in New York, New York

Selected Solo Exhibitions

1976 "Stephen Pearson: Works of Paper," Andrews University Art Center, Berrrien Springs, MI

Selected Site Works

1982 "Model Citizens Against Post-Modernism," Express Network, New York, NY
"Two Hundred Years of Architecture: A Bicentennial Salute to Los Angeles 1781–1981" (northeast corner of previous site installation with documentation), Express Network, New York, NY

1981 "Two Hundred Years of Architecture: A Bicentennial Salute to Los Angeles 1781–1981" (installation), Asher/Faure Gallery, Los Angeles, CA (secondary installation, Los Angeles Institute of Contemporary Art, CA)
"Tricks and Treats at the Wax Museum," Coney Island, NY (installation and performance)

Selected Group Exhibitions

1983 "Out of Towners," Project Space, Eugene, OR
1982 "Franklin Furnace, Sweet Art Sale," Ronald Feldman Gallery, New York, NY
1981 "Small Works Show," Washington Square Gallery, New York, NY
1980 "Geometric Abstraction," The Brooklyn Law School, NY
1973 "National Show," The Butler Museum, Youngstown, OH
1972 "All Michigan," Flint Art Institute, MI

WORKS IN THE EXHIBITION

"Two Hundred Years of Architecture: A Bicentennial Salute to Los Angeles 1781–1981," 1981

Three color photographs, 14" × 9" (two) and 9" × 14" (one): detail views of 794 identical houses, 8" × 11" × 8" each; pine clapboard siding and metal roofing
Site: Malibu Cliffs (between Paradise Cove and Point Dume)
Lent by the artist
Photographed by Stephen Pearson

Five of the 794 identical houses
Courtesy of Asher/Faure Gallery, Los Angeles, CA

"Two Hundred Years of Architecture: A Bicentennial Salute to Los Angeles 1781–1981" (preliminary installation), 1980 (plate 36)**

Color photograph, 14" × 9": detail view of 550 identical houses, 8" × 11" × 8" each; pine clapboard siding and metal roofing
Site: Malibu Cliffs (between Paradise Cove and Point Dume)
Lent by the artist
Photographed by Stephen Pearson

STEPHEN PEARSON

PLATES 37 AND 38   *BUM SHELTER (TWO VIEWS)*, 1979

STATEMENT

I try to think of scale of a work in terms of its social implications and in terms of the questions it asks, instead of physical size. There is such a thing as "social scale" of a work which is independent of size or grandiosity, and bears no relationship to the amount of work put in to accomplish the piece. Roughly speaking,

social complexity = social scale

Jon Peterson, 1983

SELECTED BIOGRAPHY

Born in Stillwater, Minnesota, 1945
Lives in Los Angeles, California

Selected Honors

1980   National Endowment for the Arts, Artist's Fellowship
1976   Teaching Fellowship, Otis Art Institute, Los Angeles, CA

Selected Solo Exhibitions

1980   Protetch-McIntosh Gallery, Washington, D.C.
1979,   Newspace Gallery, Los Angeles, CA
78,77,
76
1975   Manitoba Museum of Fine Arts, San Francisco, CA

Selected Site Works

1983   "Boom Town Shelter," Houston Art Festival, TX
1982   "Hieroglyph House," Foundation for Art Resources, Los Angeles, CA
1981   "Inflatable Shelters," Washington Project for the Arts, Washington, D.C.
       "Truax (Bless Them All)," Madison Art Center, WI
       "Bunker Hill Shelter," Los Angeles Contemporary Exhibitions, CA
1980   "Washington, D.C. Shelters" ("11th International Sculpture Conference"), Washington, D.C.
       "Santa Barbara Shelter," Santa Barbara Contemporary Art Forum, CA

Selected Group Exhibitions

1983   Houston Art Festival, TX
1982   "Transitional Use," Los Angeles, CA
1982-   "Between the Freeways," WAAM traveling museum exhibition,
81   (six U.S. museums)
1981   "Site Work: Downtown L.A.," Los Angeles Contemporary Exhibitions, CA
       "Nine and the Wall," California State University, Fullerton, CA (cat.)
       "Streetworks," Washington Project for the Arts, Washington, D.C.
1980   "Art and Architecture," Los Angeles Institute of Contemporary Art, CA
       "11th International Sculpture Conference," Washington, D.C.
       "Sculpture in California, 1975–1980," San Diego Museum of Art, CA
       "Downtown L.A. in Santa Barbara," Santa Barbara Museum of Art, CA
1976   "All California Show," Laguna Beach Museum of Art, CA

WORKS IN THE EXHIBITION

"Bum Shelter," 1979*
20" × 35" × 72," wood and fiberglass
Downtown Los Angeles, CA

"Bum Shelters" (two views), 1979 (plates 37 and 38)*
42" × 30" × 108," wood and fiberglass
Downtown Los Angeles, CA
Photographed by Jon Peterson

"Bum Shelter," 1979*
30" × 96" diameter, wood and fiberglass
Downtown Los Angeles, CA

" Bum Shelter," 1980*
40" × 48" diameter, wood and fiberglass
New York, NY

JON PETERSON

PLATE 39   *EVERYDAY MARVELS, 1983*

STATEMENT

When the child draws a circle which closes and that circle which closes is, it's the place, it's where I am, it's where I exist, it's the territory, it's my house.

The house is place, refuge; it's place of existence almost frighteningly simplistic and a statement of our great need for security in a world of change. I think that's what it really stands for—for us.

Roland Reiss, 1983

SELECTED BIOGRAPHY

Born in Chicago, Illinois, 1929
Lives in Venice, California

Selected Honors

1976 National Council on the Arts Fellowship
1970 National Council on the Arts Fellowship

Selected Solo Exhibitions

1983 Flow Ace Gallery, Los Angeles, CA
1981 Pittsburgh Arts and Crafts Center, PA
      Santa Barbara Museum of Art, CA (cat.)
1980 Ace Gallery, Vancouver, British Columbia, Canada
      Ace Gallery, Venice, CA
1978 South Alberta Art Gallery, Lethbridge, Alberta, Canada
      Calgary Museum, Alberta, Canada
1977 Los Angeles County Museum of Art, CA (cat.)
      Cirrus Gallery, Los Angeles, CA
      Chico State College, CA

Selected Group Exhibitions

1983 "L.A. Seen," University of Southern California, Los Angeles, CA
      "Day In/Day Out: Ordinary Life as a Source for Art," Freedman Gallery, Albright College, Reading, PA (cat.)
      Fuller Goldeen Gallery, San Francisco, CA
      "Cultural Excavations: Recent and Distant," Japanese American Cultural and Community Center, Los Angeles, CA (cat.)
1982 "Dokumenta 7," Kassel, West Germany (cat.)
      "One Hundred Years of California Sculpture," The Oakland Museum, CA (cat.)
      "Microcosms," Santa Barbara Contemporary Arts Forum, CA
      "20 American Artists: Sculpture, 1982," San Francisco Museum of Art, CA (cat.)
      "Imaginative Sculpture," Security Pacific Bank Plaza, Los Angeles, CA (cat.)
1981 "Art in Los Angeles—The Museum as Site: Sixteen Projects," Los Angeles County Museum of Art, CA (cat.)
      "Humor in Art," Los Angeles Institute of Contemporary Art, CA
      "The Intimate Object," The Downtown Gallery, Los Angeles, CA
1980 "Architectural Sculpture," Fine Arts Gallery, Mount St. Mary's College, Los Angeles, CA (organized by Los Angeles Institute of Contemporary Art, CA) (cat.)
      "Contemporary Art in Southern California," The High Museum of Art, Atlanta, GA
      "Tableau," Middendorf/Lane Gallery, Washington, D.C.
      "Small-Scale Sculpture," Municipal Art Gallery, Barnsdall Park, Los Angeles, CA
      "Sculpture in California, 1975-1980," San Diego Museum of Art, CA
1979 "Directions," Hirshhorn Museum and Sculpture Garden, Smithsonian Institution, Washington, D.C. (cat.)
      "Visual Musical Permutations," University of California, Irvine, CA
1979, "Rooms: Moments Remembered," Newport Harbor Art Museum,
78   Newport Beach, CA (cat.)
1978 "Miniature Narratives," University of California, San Diego, La Jolla, CA
1977 "Photographs by Southern California Painters and Sculptors," University of California, Santa Barbara, CA (cat.)
      "Miniature," California State University, Los Angeles, CA (cat.)
      "Private Images: Photographs by Sculptors," Los Angeles County Museum of Art, CA
      "Los Angeles in the Seventies," Fort Worth Art Museum, TX (cat.)
      "Attitudes," California State University, Los Angeles, CA

PLATES 40 AND 41 *THE DANCING LESSONS: CENTRIFUGAL FORCE* (TWO VIEWS), 1981

WORKS IN THE EXHIBITION

"Everyday Marvels," 1983 (plate 39)
12" × 24" × 24," mixed media
Courtesy of Flow Ace Gallery, Los Angeles, CA
Photograph courtesy of Flow Ace Gallery, Los Angeles, CA

"The Dancing Lessons: Centrifugal Force" (two views), 1981 (plates 40 and 41)**
12" × 24" × 24," mixed media
Lent by Gail and Barry Berkus
Photograph courtesy of Flow Ace Gallery, Los Angeles, CA

"The Morality Plays: The Moral Rights of Objects," 1981*
12" × 24" × 24," mixed media

ROLAND REISS

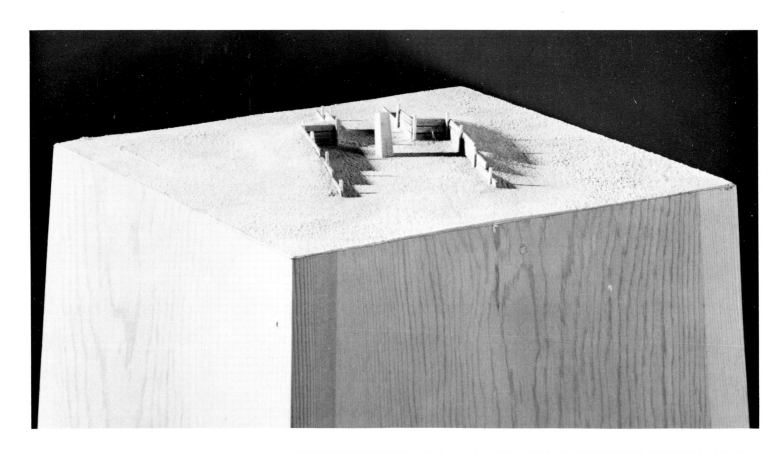

PLATE 42   *DESERT IMAGE: BUTTRESS SYSTEM PROJECTING COLUMN, 1979*
PLATE 43   *DESERT IMAGE: WITH TENT ON-SITE, 1979*

STATEMENT

The essence of my work lies in the interplay of materials, formal elements, and content—always coming together into the whole through the creative process. I'm a builder, and I enjoy "making" the piece, while at the same time feeling the fantasy take shape as I work on large-scale site sculpture or on smaller work.

I am a landscape artist. Rather than recording the natural, I seek to use nature by taking the landscape as my visual theme within which to treat surfaces, make marks, paint colors, manipulate scale, and play shapes one on another. In terms of content, I take our universal relationship with the land—not to tell a story, but, rather, to suggest its familiar experience. I am presenting an illusion that will lead one to ponder rather than to know.

From Sam Richardson, *Sam Richardson: Landscape Constructs* (Santa Barbara Museum of Art, 1981), n.p.

SELECTED BIOGRAPHY

Born in Oakland, California, 1934
Lives in Oakland, California

Selected Solo Exhibitions
1982 Shasta College, Redding, CA
      San Jose Museum of Art, CA
      Klein Gallery, Chicago, IL
1981 Santa Barbara Museum of Art, CA (cat.)
1980 Hansen Fuller Goldeen Gallery, San Francisco, CA
      Janus Gallery, Los Angeles, CA
1979 Hansen Fuller Goldeen Gallery, San Francisco, CA
      San Jose Museum of Art, CA
      Boehm Gallery, Palomar College, San Marcos, CA
      Wordworks Gallery, San Jose, CA
1978 University of California, Davis, CA
      San Jose Museum of Art, CA
      The Oakland Museum, CA
1977 California State University, Fullerton, CA (cat.)
1975 M.H. deYoung Memorial Museum, San Francisco, CA
      Martha Jackson Gallery, New York, NY

Selected Site Works and Commissions
1982 City Administration Building, Livermore, CA
      Mr. and Mrs. George Norton, La Honda, CA
      The Koll Company, San Jose, CA
1981 Santa Barbara Museum of Art, CA
1980 Hansen Fuller Goldeen Gallery, San Francisco, CA
      Janus Gallery, Los Angeles, CA
1979 Wordworks Gallery, San Jose, CA
1977 California State University, Fullerton, CA
1976 Dallas Museum of Fine Art, TX
      Martha Jackson Gallery West, New York, NY
1975 M.H. deYoung Memorial Museum, San Francisco, CA
1974 The Oakland Museum, CA
1973 Mills College, Oakland, CA
      The Denver Art Museum, CO

Selected Group Exhibitions
1983 "Resource/Reservoir: CCAC: 75 Years," San Francisco Museum of Modern Art, CA
1982 "Shoebox Sculpture Exhibition," University of Hawaii Art Gallery, Honolulu, HI
      "A Private Vision—Contemporary Art from the Graham Gund Collection," Museum of Fine Arts, Boston, MA (cat.)
      "The West as Art: Changing Perceptions of Western Art in California Collections," Palm Springs Desert Museum, CA (cat.)
      "Mile of Sculpture: Art EXPO," Chicago Sculpture Society, Navy Pier, Chicago, IL
      "100 Years of California Sculpture," The Oakland Museum, CA
      "Northern California Art of the Sixties," de Saisset Museum, University of Santa Clara, CA
1981 "Alumni Exhibition," California College of Arts and Crafts, Oakland, CA

"California: The State of Landscape, 1872–1981," Newport Harbor Art Museum, Newport Beach, CA (cat.)
"Polychrome," Hansen Fuller Goldeen Gallery, San Francisco, CA
"Inaugural Exhibition," Klein Gallery, Chicago, IL
"Then and Now: 1960–1980," Hansen Fuller Goldeen Gallery, San Francisco, CA
1980 "Painted Sculpture," Palo Alto Cultural Center, CA
      "Artists of the Pacific Coast States," The Vice President's House, Washington, D.C.
1978 "California 3×8 Twice," Honolulu Academy of Arts, HI
1977 "Landscape: New Views," Herbert F. Johnson Museum of Art, Cornell University, Ithaca, NY
1977- "Painting and Sculpture in California: The Modern Era," San
76   Francisco Museum of Modern Art, CA (circulated: National Collection of Fine Arts, Smithsonian Institution, Washington, D.C.)
       "California Bay Area Art—Update," Huntsville Museum of Art, AL
       "A Sense of Scale," The Oakland Museum, CA
1975 "Martha Jackson Gallery Collection," Koehler Art Center, San Antonio, TX
       "Small Scale Environments," The Art Institute of Chicago, IL
       "Response to the Environment," University Art Gallery, Rutgers University, New Brunswick, NJ
       "Contemporary California Artists," Utah Museum of Fine Art, University of Utah, Salt Lake City, UT
       "California Landscape," The Oakland Museum, CA
       "The Sculptor as Draughtsman," JPL Fine Arts, London, England
1974 "Public Sculpture, Urban Environment," The Oakland Museum, CA
1973 "First Sculpture Invitational," Palo Alto Cultural Center, CA
1972 "Topography of Nature," Institute of Contemporary Art," University of Pennsylvania, Philadelphia, PA
       "West Coast Sculpture Invitational," Stanford University Art Gallery, Palo Alto, CA
1971 "Centennial Show," San Francisco Art Institute, CA
       "Spray," Santa Barbara Museum of Art, CA
       "Martha Jackson Gallery Collection," Seibu Store, Tokyo, Japan

WORKS IN THE EXHIBITION

"Desert Image: Buttress System Projecting Column," 1979 (plate 42)
36"×8¾"×8¾," leather and wood
Courtesy of Fuller Goldeen Gallery, San Francisco, CA
Photographed by M. Lee Fatherree

"Desert Image: With Tent On-Site," 1979 (plate 43)**
36"×8¾"×8¾," leather, wood and string
Courtesy of Fuller Goldeen Gallery, San Francisco, CA
Photographed by M. Lee Fatherree

SAM RICHARDSON

PLATE 44   *SAN FERNANDO VALLEY,* 1965

84

STATEMENT

The buildings out here are like the ethnics that inhabit them—they are all mixing and mutating. A hundred years from now there will be some gorgeous mono-ethnic race living here in mono-ethnic buildings.

Edward Ruscha, 1983

SELECTED BIOGRAPHY
Born in Omaha, Nebraska, 1937
Lives in Los Angeles, California

Selected Honors
Purchase Award, "Biennial of Graphic Art," Moderna Galerija, Ljunjana, Yugoslavia

Selected Solo Exhibitions
1983 "Route 66," Philadelphia, PA
Bernard Jacobson Gallery, Los Angeles, CA
Cirrus Editions, Ltd., Los Angeles, CA
Galleria del Cavallino, Venice, Italy
1982 "The Works of Edward Ruscha," San Francisco Museum of Modern Art, CA (circulated: Whitney Museum of American Art, New York, NY; Vancouver Art Gallery, Vancouver, British Columbia, Canada; Contemporary Arts Museum, Houston, TX; Los Angeles County Museum of Art, CA) (cat.)
John Berggruen Gallery, San Francisco, CA
Flow Ace Gallery, Los Angeles, CA
Castelli Uptown, New York, NY
1981 Leo Castlelli, New York, NY
ARCO Center for Visual Art, Los Angeles, CA
Ace Gallery, Vancouver, British Columbia, Canada
1980 Portland Center for the Visual Arts, OR
Ace Gallery, Venice, CA
Foster Goldstrom, San Francisco, CA
1979 Richard Hines Gallery, Seattle, WA
Texas Gallery, Houston, TX
Ink, Zurich, Switzerland
1978 Galerie Ricke, Cologne, West Germany
MTL Gallery, Brussels, Belgium
Rudiger Schottle, Munich, West Germany
1977 University of Lethbridge, Alberta, Ontario, Canada (circulated: University of Calgary Art Gallery, Alberta, Ontario, Canada)
1976 Stedelijk Museum, Amsterdam, The Netherlands
Albright-Knox Art Gallery, Buffalo, NY
Institute of Contemporary Art, London, England
Sable Castelli Gallery Ltd., Toronto, Ontario, Canada
1975 Galerie Ricke, Cologne, West Germany (circulated: The Arts Council of Great Britain, twelve Council member galleries)
Ace Gallery, Vancouver, British Columbia, Canada
Los Angeles Institute of Contemporary Art, CA
Matrix Gallery, Wadsworth Atheneum, Hartford, CT

Selected Group Exhibitions
1983 "Drawings by Painters," The Oakland Museum, CA
"Cirrus Editions, Ltd./A Retrospective View," Stephen Wirtz Gallery, San Francisco, CA
"L.A. Seen," University Art Galleries, University of Southern California, Los Angeles, CA
"1984—A Preview," Ronald Feldman Fine Arts, New York, NY
"Drawing Conclusions," Daniel Weinberg Gallery, Los Angeles, CA
"Fire and Water," Neil G. Ovsey Gallery, Los Angeles, CA
"Perspectives of Landscape," Fuller Goldeen Gallery, San Francisco, CA
1982 "The West as Art: Changing Perceptions of Western Art in California Collections," Palm Springs Desert Museum, CA (cat.)
"Facons de Peindre," Musée Rath, Geneva, Switzerland
"Contemporary Los Angeles Artists," Nagoya City Museum, Japan
"Los Angeles Art: An Exhibition of Contemporary Paintings," Municipal Art Gallery, Barnsdall Park, Los Angeles, CA
1981 "The Americans: The Landscape," Contemporary Arts Museum, Houston, TX
"Major Works," Richard Hines Gallery, Seattle, WA
"Humor in Art," Los Angeles Institute of Contemporary Art, CA
"California: The State of Landscape, 1872–1981," Newport Harbor Art Museum, Newport Beach, CA (cat.)

"Contemporary American Prints and Drawings," National Gallery of Art, Washington, D.C.
"Forty Famous Californians," Judith Christian Gallery, New York, NY
1980 "8th International Poster Biennial," Warsaw, Poland
"Printed Art, A View of Two Decades," The Museum of Modern Art, New York, NY
"Pier + Ocean: Construction in the Art of the Seventies," Hayward Gallery, London, England (circulated: Rijksmuseum Kröller-Müller, Otterlo, The Netherlands) (cat.)
"Contemporary Art in Southern California," The High Museum of Art, Atlanta, GA
"AZ 1970-ES Evek Uj Amerikai Festeszete," Hungary (organized by The New Museum, New York, NY)
1979 "With a Certain Smile," Ink, Zurich, Switzerland
"Artists and Books: The Literal Use of Time," Ulrich Museum of Art, Wichita State University, KS
"Twentieth-Century Drawings from the Whitney Museum of American Art," Whitney Museum of American Art, New York, NY
1978 "Three Generations: Studies in Collage," Margo Leavin Gallery, Los Angeles, CA
"Retrospective of the Biennales of Paris, 1959–1975," The Seibu Museum of Art, Tokyo, Japan
"Aesthetics of Graffiti," San Francisco Museum of Modern Art, CA
"Words Words," Museum Bochum, Bochum, West Germany
1977 "The Last Time I Saw Ferus," Newport Harbor Art Museum, Newport Beach, CA
"California Images," Whitney Museum of American Art, New York, NY (film "Miracle")
"10e Biennale de Paris," National Foundation of Plastic Art, Paris, France
"First Biennial of American Graphics," Municipal Museum of Graphic Art, Maracaibo, Venezuela
"Eyes and Ears Billboard Project," Wilshire Boulevard at Los Angeles County Museum of Art, CA
"100+, Current Directions in Southern California Art," Los Angeles Institute of Contemporary Art, CA
"Biennial of Graphic Art," Moderna Galerija, Ljunjuna, Yugoslavia
"Illusion and Reality," The Western Australian Art Gallery, Sydney, Australia (circulated)

WORK IN THE EXHIBITION

"San Fernando Valley," 1965 (plate 44)*
14⅛" × 22⅝," graphite on paper
Photographed by Susan Haller

85　　　　　　　　　　　　　　　　　　EDWARD RUSCHA

PLATE 45   *THE CURTAIN*, 1974

86

STATEMENT

In reference to my sculpture and the relationship between the seated figure and the architectural space, years ago I noticed that people were very deeply moved by the nature of the place and space they were in. If I was going to make a sculpture, I felt I had to select a segment of an architectural place and reconstruct it, and then somehow put the model in that place doing something quite normal and everyday. In order to intensify the feeling, I would carefully select, for example, a chair, a stool, a counter, and use the same kind of lighting, such as a cold fluorescent or incandescent light like in a diner or restaurant. Then I would very carefully shape the empty air, the normal objects and the gesture in the human body in order to translate the posture and somehow lock into that place, such as in "The Restaurant Window." The transparent pane of glass acts as an impenetrable barrier between the two people. There is absolutely no contact between these people, the geometry of the place and the coldness of the place. It would shrivel any possibility of human contact.

George Segal, 1983

SELECTED BIOGRAPHY
Born in New York, New York, 1924
Lives in North Brunswick, New Jersey

Selected Honors
Honorary Doctorate, Rutgers University, NY
State Department cultural exchange visit with the Soviet Union

Selected Solo Exhibitions
1983 The Israel Museum, Jerusalem, Israel
1982 Sidney Janis Gallery, New York, NY
      Seibu Museum, Tokyo, Japan
      Takanawa Museum, Japan
1978- Walker Art Center, Minneapolis, MN (circulated: Museum of
77   Modern Art, San Francisco, CA; Whitney Museum of American Art, New York, NY)
1977 Sidney Janis Gallery, New York, NY
1967 Sidney Janis Gallery, New York, NY
1965 Sidney Janis Gallery, New York, NY
1964 Green Gallery, New York, NY

Selected Group Exhibitions
1983 "Expressionist Image: Pollock to Today," Sidney Janis Gallery, New York, NY (circulated: Whitney Museum of American Art at Philip Morris, New York, NY) (cat.)
      "Recent Work," Sidney Janis Gallery, New York, NY
1982 "Real, Really Real, Super Real," Museum of Fine Arts, San Antonio, TX (cat.)
      "Exhibition of Work by Newly Elected Members and Recipients of Honors and Awards," American Academy of Arts and Letters, New York, NY
      "Contemporary Realism Since 1960," Pennsylvania Academy of the Fine Arts, Philadelphia, PA (circulated: The Virginia Museum of Fine Arts, Norfolk, VA; The Oakland Museum, CA)
      "Flat and Figurative 20th Century Wall Sculpture," Zabriskie Gallery, New York, NY
1968 "The Sidney and Harriet Janis Collection," The Museum of Modern Art, New York, NY
1967 "Dine–Oldenburg–Segal," Art Gallery of Ontario, Canada (circulated: Art Gallery of Toronto, Ontario, Canada; Albright-Knox Art Gallery, Buffalo, NY)
      "American Sculpture of the Sixties," Los Angeles County Museum of Art, CA (circulated: Philadelphia Museum of Art, PA)
      "Focus on Light," New Jersey State Museum, Trenton, NJ
      "Environment U.S.A.: 1957–1967," organized by Rose Art Museum, Brandeis University, Waltham, MA, for the American section of the IX São Paulo Bienal, Brazil

"7 for '67," City Art Museum of St. Louis, MO
"Art of the Sixties," The Museum of Modern Art, New York, NY
"Protest and Hope: An Exhibition on Civil Rights and Viet Nam," New School Art Center, New York, NY
"Homage to Marilyn Monroe," Sidney Janis Gallery, New York, NY
"Original Pop Art," Städtische Kunstaustellung, Gelsenkirchen, West Germany
"A Look at American Art: Yesterday and Today," Bambergers, Newark, NJ (circulated: New York State Fair, Syracuse, NY)
1966 "Crosscurrents in American Art," Cordier and Ekstrom, New York, NY
"The Harry N. Abrams Family Collection," The Jewish Museum, New York, NY
"68th Annual American Exhibition," The Art Institute of Chicago, IL
"Eight Sculptors: The Ambiguous Image," Walker Art Center, Minneapolis, MN
"Art of the United States 1670–1966," Whitney Museum of American Art, New York, NY
"Environmental Paintings and Constructions," The Jewish Museum, New York, NY
"Pop Art aus U.S.A.," Hans R. Neuendorf Gallery, Hamburg, West Germany
"The Found Object: Can It Be Art," Institute of Contemporary Art, Boston, MA
"Recent Still-Life," Museum of Art, Rhode Island School of Design, Providence, RI
"Walter K. Gutman Collection," Bowdoin College Museum of Art, Brunswick, ME

WORKS IN THE EXHIBITION

"The Curtain," 1974 (plate 45) *
84" × 39" × 32," plaster and mixed media
Courtesy of Sidney Janis Gallery, New York, NY
Photograph by O.E. Nelson, courtesy of Sidney Janis Gallery, New York, NY

"The Restaurant Window," 1967*
72" × 75" × 47," plaster, plastic, metal and wood with film

"Robert & Ethel Scull," 1965*
96" × 72" × 72," plaster, wood, canvas and cloth

"Cinema," 1963*
118" × 96" × 39," plaster, metal, plexiglass and fluorescent light

GEORGE SEGAL

PLATE 46 *GENERATOR (A STUDY IN COPPER AND GRAY),* 1981

88

STATEMENT

I like paintings as big as buildings. Since 1969 my major works have been murals. I prefer that the murals don't just sit there. I like them to be focal points and qualifiers for the environments they occupy. Los Angeles is a good city for murals. Sometimes a painting on an L.A. building has a greater claim to reality than the architecture around it.

Terry Schoonhoven, 1983

SELECTED BIOGRAPHY

Born in Freeport, Illinois, 1945
Lives in Los Angeles, California

Selected Solo Exhibitions

1982 "Vapor Dreams in L.A.—Terry Schoonhoven's Empty Stage," Retrospective, California State University, Long Beach, CA (cat.)
1980 "Downtown Los Angeles Underwater and Other Proposals," ARCO Center for Visual Art, Los Angeles, CA
Hogarth Gallery, Sydney, Australia
1977- "Terry Schoonhoven Paints a Mural for the Newport Harbor Art
76 Museum," Newport Harbor Art Museum, Newport Beach, CA (circulated: Colorado Springs Fine Arts Center, CO; University Art Gallery, Tempe, AZ; E.B. Crocker Art Center, Sacramento, CA; Art Gallery, California State University, Chico, CA)

Selected Solo Site Works

1984- Olympic Games Mural, Downtown Los Angeles, CA
83
1982 "Doumani House Murals," 12'×12' (skylight); 39'×39'×36,' (niche), Venice, CA
1981 "Passage," 14'×250,' San Antonio Museum of Art, TX
"Generator (A Study in Copper and Gray)," 11'×12,' Ahmanson Gallery facade, Los Angeles County Museum of Art, CA
1981- "Pasadena Painting," 6,000 square feet, Pasadena, CA
80
1979 "Study in Silver," 10'×32,' Century City, CA
1979- "St. Charles Painting," 50'×100,' Venice, CA
78
1976 "No River," 24'×35,' Minneapolis, MN
"Adobe Gillis," 14'×40,' Thousand Oaks, CA
"Study in Chrome and Gray," 14'×10,' Venice, CA
1975 "S.P.Q.R.," 9'×18,' University of California, Los Angeles, CA

Los Angeles Fine Arts Squad Site Works

1973- "Ghost Town," 14'×50,' Thousand Oaks, CA
72
1971 "Hippie Know How," 19'×50,' Paris, France
"Isle of California," 42'×65,' Los Angeles, CA
"Black Submarine," 9'×40,' Newport Beach, CA
1970 "Venice in the Snow," 20'×70,' Venice, CA
1970- "Beverly Hills Siddhartha," 20'×300,' Beverly Hills, CA
69
1969 "Brooks Street Painting," 19'×25,' Venice, CA

Selected Group Exhibitions

1982 "Six Walls—Downtown," Koplin Gallery, Los Angeles, CA
1981 "Art in Los Angeles—The Museum as Site: Sixteen Projects," Los Angeles County Museum of Art, CA (cat.)
"California: The State of Landscape, 1872–1981," Newport Harbor Art Museum, Newport Beach, CA (cat.)
"Humor in Art," Los Angeles Institute of Contemporary Art, CA
1980 "L.A. Artists Look at L.A.," Municipal Art Gallery, Barnsdall Park, Los Angeles, CA
1978 "Five L.A. Wall Painters," The Arts Center, Sylmar, CA
1977 "Illusion and Reality" (circulated by the Australian Council throughout Australia)
"Spring Rites," Art Rental Gallery, Los Angeles County Museum of Art, CA
1976 "L.A. 2001," Image and the Myth Gallery, Beverly Hills, CA
"The River: Images of the Mississippi," Walker Art Center, Minneapolis, MN
1975 "A Drawing Show," Newport Harbor Art Museum, Newport Beach, CA
Betty Gold Gallery, Los Angeles, CA

WORK IN THE EXHIBITION

"Generator (A Study in Copper and Gray)," 1981 (plate 46)*
11'×12,' acrylic mural
Site: Ahmanson Gallery facade, Los Angeles County Museum of Art, CA
Photograph courtesy of Los Angeles County Museum of Art, Photography Department

TERRY SCHOONHOVEN

PLATE 47   *UNTITLED,* 1979

90

STATEMENT

I took the metaphor of the house and isolated it. I took a house and plopped it in the middle of a field—not a grassy, green field—I mean an area. . . . This house is not engaged so much with the space that it actually occupies, but functions in a much more psychologically determined space instead. It is removed. It is very sentimental. It gives a real sense of isolation. This small, longing house is removed from you, but you can feel it.

The first house sat directly on the floor—it was competing with the space of the room, trying to insist on itself in relation to the walls and the ceiling of the room. . . . Putting the house on the field condensed what was outside into the space of the piece. The base was a way of getting it up in the air. I wanted something light and airy. I wanted to have an overview of it. Then this whole area can extend out and magnify the image. It gives it a viscosity.

Joel Shapiro in *Joel Shapiro* (New York, Whitney Museum of American Art, 1982), p. 98.

SELECTED BIOGRAPHY

Born in New York, New York
Lives in New York, New York

Selected Honor
1975 National Endowment for the Arts, Artist's Fellowship

Selected Solo Exhibitions
1983- "Joel Shapiro," Whitney Museum of American Art, New York,
82   NY (circulated: Dallas Museum of Fine Arts, TX; The Art Gallery of Ontario, Toronto, Canada; La Jolla Museum of Contemporary Art, CA) (cat.)
1982 "Joel Shapiro: Recent Sculptures and Drawings," Yarlow/Salzman Gallery, Toronto, Ontario, Canada
      "Joel Shapiro," Portland Center for the Visual Arts, OR
      "Joel Shapiro: Drawings," Paula Cooper Gallery, New York, NY
1981 "Joel Shapiro: Recent Sculpture," Daniel Weinberg Gallery, San Francisco, CA
      "Joel Shapiro," The Israel Museum, Jerusalem, Israel (cat.)
      William Hayes Ackland Art Museum, University of North Carolina, Chapel Hill, NC
1981, "Joel Shapiro: Sculpture," Galerie Mukai, Tokyo, Japan (cat.)
80,79
1980, "Joel Shapiro," Paula Cooper Gallery, New York, NY
79,77
1980 "Joel Shapiro: Sculpture and Drawing," Whitechapel Art Gallery, London, England (circulated: Museum Haus Lange, Kredfeld, West Germany; Moderna Museet, Stockholm, Sweden) (cat.)
      Asher/Faure Gallery, Los Angeles
      Moderna Museet, Stockholm, Sweden
1980, "Joel Shapiro," Galerie Aronowitsch, Stockholm, Sweden
77
1979, "Joel Shapiro," Galerie Nancy Gillespie–Elisabeth de Laage, Paris,
77   France
1978 "Joel Shapiro," Galerie M., Bochum, West Germany
1977 "Joel Shapiro: Recent Sculpture," Max Protetch Gallery, Washington, D.C.
1976 "Joel Shapiro," Museum of Contemporary Art, Chicago, IL (cat.)
1976, "Joel Shapiro," Paula Cooper Gallery, New York, NY
75,74
1974 "Works by Joel Shapiro," Galleria Salvatore Ala, Milan, Italy
1974, Paula Cooper Gallery, New York, NY
72,70
1973 "Joel Shapiro," The Clocktower, The Institute for Art and Urban Resources, New York, NY

Selected Group Exhibitions
1983 "Entering the Eighties: Selections from the Permanent Collection of the Whitney Museum of American Art," Whitney Museum of American Art at Fairfield County, Stamford, CT

"Twentieth Century Sculpture: Statements of Form," Whitney Museum of American Art at Philip Morris, New York, NY
"Back to the USA," Rheinisches Landesmuseum Bonn, West Germany (circulated: Kunstmuseum Luzern; Wurttembergischer Kunstverein, Stuttgart, West Germany)
1982 "Great Big Drawings," Hayden Gallery, Massachusetts Institute of Technology, Cambridge, MA
      "Twenty American Artists: Sculpture 1982," San Francisco Museum of Modern Art, CA (cat.)
      "Dokumenta 7," Kassel, West Germany (cat.)
      "Seventy-fourth American Exhibition," The Art Institute of Chicago, IL (cat.)
      "PostMINIMALism," The Aldrich Museum of Contemporary Art, Ridgefield, CT
1981 "Drawings from Georgia Collection, 19th and 20th Centuries," The High Museum of Art, Atlanta, GA
      "Drawings: Joel Shapiro, Jennifer Bartlett, Elizabeth Murray," Galerie Mukai, Tokyo, Japan
      "The Whitney Biennial Exhibition of Painting and Sculpture," Whitney Museum of American Art, New York, NY
      "Drawing Distinctions: American Drawings of the Seventies," (circulated: Louisiana Museum of Modern Art, Humlebaek, Denmark; Kunsthalle Basel, Switzerland; Stadtische Gallerie im Lenbachaus, Munich, West Germany; Wilhelm-Hack-Museum, Ludwig-schafen, West Germany) (cat.)
      "Bestandsaufrahme, Tatig Keitsberight einer Galerie," Galerie M., Bochum, West Germany
      "Trois Dimensions: Sept Americans," Galerie Gillespie–Laage–Solomon, Paris, France
      "The Image of the House in Contemporary Art," University of Houston, Lawndale Annex, TX (cat.)
      "Figuratively Sculpting," P.S. 1, The Institute for Art and Urban Resources, Long Island City, NY
1980 "Nature du Dessin," Musée National d'Art Moderne, Centre National d'Art et de Culture Georges Pompidou, Paris, France
      "Drawings: The Pluralist Decade," 39th Venice Biennale, United States Pavilion, Italy (circulated: Institute of Contemporary Art, University of Pennsylvania, Philadelphia, PA; Museum of Contemporary Art, Chicago, IL) (cat.)
      "Architectural Sculpture," Los Angeles Institute of Contemporary Art, CA (cat.)
      "Contemporary Sculpture: Selections from the Collection of The Museum of Modern Art," The Museum of Modern Art, New York, NY
      "The Whitney Biennial Exhibition of Painting and Sculpture," Whitney Museum of American Art, New York, NY

WORKS IN THE EXHIBITION

"Untitled," 1982*
4" × 13½" × 11," bronze

"Untitled," 1979 (plate 47)
2¹³⁄₁₆" × 8¾" × 6¹¹⁄₁₆," cast bronze and black lacquer
Lent by Roselyne and Richard Swig
Photographed by M. Lee Fatherree

JOEL SHAPIRO

PLATE 48   *PENCIL HOUSE ON A PALETTE,* 1981

STATEMENT

Houses have unknown histories. I have been using the house as an image in my art since 1966. At first, I portrayed interiors of houses, and then began using the exterior as an image or symbol. The house to me represents not only a container in which people live, but also a container from which they can be absent.

Richard Shaw, 1983

SELECTED BIOGRAPHY

Born in Hollywood, California, 1941
Lives in Fairfax, California

Selected Solo Exhibitions

1982   Boise Gallery of Art, ID
       Mendel Art Gallery and Civic Conservatory, Saskatoon, Saskatchewan, Canada
       The Greenberg Gallery, St. Louis, MO
1981   Newport Harbor Art Museum, Newport Beach, CA
       San Jose Museum of Art, CA
       Belson-Brown Gallery, Ketchum, ID
1980   Allan Frumkin Gallery, New York, NY
1979   Braunstein Gallery, San Francisco, CA
       Michael Berger Gallery, Pittsburgh, PA
1977   Jacquelyn Anhalt Gallery, Los Angeles, CA
1976   Braunstein/Quay Gallery, New York, NY
       Braunstein/Quay Gallery, San Francisco, CA
1974   E.G. Gallery, Kansas City, MO
1973   San Francisco Museum of Modern Art, CA
1973, Quay Gallery, San Francisco, CA
71,70

Selected Group Exhibitions

1983   "Illusion Reality: Trompe L'oeil," Galerie Alain Blondel, Paris, France
       "Contemporary TrompeL'oeil Painting and Sculpture," Boise Gallery of Art, ID (circulated)
1982   "Pacific Currents/Ceramics 1982," San Jose Museum of Art, CA
1982- "Ceramic Sculpture: Six Artists," Whitney Museum of American
81   Art, New York, NY (circulated: San Francisco Museum of Art, CA)
1981   "The Whitney Biennial Exhibition of Painting and Sculpture," Whitney Museum of American Art, New York, NY
       "California: The State of Landscape, 1872–1981," Newport Harbor Art Museum, Newport Beach, CA (cat.)
1981- "Reality of Illusion," The Denver Art Museum and the University
79   Galleries of the University of Southern California (circulated)
1980   "American Porcelain: New Expressions in an Ancient Art," Renwick Gallery of the National Collection of Fine Arts, Smithsonian Institution, Washington, D.C. (circulated)
1980- "A Century of Ceramics in the U.S., 1878–1978," Everson
79   Museum of Art of Syracuse and Onondaga County, NY (circulated: Renwick Gallery of the National Collection of Fine Arts, Smithsonian Institution, Washington, D.C.)
1979   "West Coast Clay Spectrum," Security Pacific Bank, Los Angeles, CA
       "West Coast Ceramics," Stedelijk Museum, Amsterdam, The Netherlands
1978   "Clay from Molds: Multiples, Altered Castings, Combinations," John Michael Kohler Arts Center, Sheboygan, WI
1977- "Painting and Sculpture in California: The Modern Era," San
76   San Francisco Museum of Art, CA (circulated: National Collection of Fine Arts, Smithsonian Institution, Washington, D.C.)
1976   "Illusionistic Realism," Laguna Beach Museum of Art, CA
1975   "Clay, U.S.A.," Fendrick Gallery, Washington, D.C.
1974   "Clay," Whitney Museum Downtown Branch, New York, NY
1973   "Robert Hudson/Richard Shaw," E.G. Gallery, Kansas City, MO
1972   "A Decade of Ceramic Art: 1962–1972, from the Collection of Professor and Mrs. Joseph Monsen," San Francisco Museum of Art, CA
1972- "Contemporary Ceramic Art: Canada, U.S.A., Mexico and
71   Japan," The National Museum of Modern Art, Kyoto, Japan
1970   "Annual Exhibition," Whitney Museum of American Art, New York, NY

1969   "Objects U.S.A.," National Collection of Fine Arts, Smithsonian Institution, Washington, D.C.
1965   "New Ceramic Forms," Museum of Contemporary Crafts, New York, NY

WORKS IN THE EXHIBITION

"Vertical Penal House," 1982*
8½" × 13" × 6½," porcelain with decal overglaze

"Ledger with House," 1981
6" × 13¾" × 9," porcelain with decal overglaze
Lent by Braunstein Gallery, San Francisco, CA

"Pencil House on a Palette," 1981 (plate 48)
5½" × 12¾" × 15," porcelain with decal overglaze
Lent by Ruth and Todd Braunstein
Photographed by Schopplein Studio

"Quaddy Head," 1981*
34" × 20½" × 19¾," porcelain with decal overglaze

"Warren Walter, William," 1981*
59" × 27" × 12," porcelain with decal overglaze

RICHARD SHAW

PLATE 49   *ON-SITE INSTALLATION,* 1982

94

STATEMENT

The history for me and for them—the Little People—is an endless invocation of *to dwell*, to make homes. Making a dwelling is like building a campfire: you inhabit yourself in one particular place now. . . . I'm interested in how organisms live, the ways in which they live. It's not just the objects, it's the means of inhabitation—how they go about it.

Charles Simonds in Christopher Lyon, "Charles Simonds: A Profile," *Images & Issues,* vol. 2, Spring 1982, pp. 56–58.

SELECTED BIOGRAPHY

Born in New York, New York, 1945
Lives in New York, New York

Selected Solo Exhibitions

1983   "Charles Simonds," The Solomon R. Guggenheim Museum, New York, NY (brochure)
Fort Worth Art Museum, TX
"Charles Simonds," Los Angeles County Museum of Art, CA
1982- "Charles Simonds," Museum of Contemporary Art, Chicago,
81   IL (cat.)
1980   Beaumont-May Gallery, Dartmouth College, Hanover, NH
California State University, Los Angeles, CA
1979   Wallraf-Richartz Museum, Museum Ludwig, Cologne, West Germany
National-galerie, West Berlin, West Germany
Musée de l'Abbaye Sainte-Croix, Les Sables–d'Olonne, France
"Circles and Towers Growing," Galerie Baudoin Lebon, Paris, France (cat.)
Centre d'Art Contemporain, Geneva, Switzerland
"Floating Cities," Samangallery, Genoa, Italy
1978   "Charles Simonds: Floating Cities and Other Architectures," organized with the Berliner Kunstlerprogramm des Deutschen Akademischen Austauschdienstes (DAAD), Westfälischer Kunstverein, Münster, West Germany, and Bonn Kunstverein, Bonn, West Germany (cat.)
1976   "Projects: Charles Simonds: Picaresque Landscape," The Museum of Modern Art, New York, NY (circulated: New York Public Library, Tompkins Square, NY)
1976, Centre National d'Art et de Culture Georges Pompidou, Paris,
75   France
"Charles Simonds: Demeures et Mythologies," Samangallery, Genoa, Italy (cat.)

Selected Group Exhibitions

1981   "Architecture by Artists," Rosa Esman Gallery, New York, NY
"Mythos & Ritual in der Kunst der 70er Jahre," Kunsthaus Zürich, Switzerland
1980   "Architectural References," Vancouver Art Gallery, British Columbia, Canada (cat.)
"Pier + Ocean: Construction in the Art of the Seventies," Hayward Gallery, London, England (circulated: Rijksmuseum Kröller-Müller, Otterlo, The Netherlands) (cat.)
"11th International Sculpture Conference," Washington, D.C. (cat.)
"Charles Simonds," California State University, Los Angeles, CA (cat.)
"Architectural Sculpture," California State University, Los Angeles, CA (organized by Los Angeles Institute of Contemporary Art, CA) (cat.)
1980- "Supershow," organized by Independent Curators, Inc., New
79   York, NY (circulated) (cat.)
"Maska, Tents, Vessels, Talismans," Institute of Contemporary Art, University of Pennsylvania, Philadelphia, PA
1979   "Contemporary Sculpture: Selections from the Collection of The Museum of Modern Art," The Museum of Modern Art, New York, NY (cat.)
"Ten Artists/Artists' Space," Neuberger Museum, State University of New York, College at Purchase, NY
1978   "Spring Festival," The American Center, Paris, organized by Galerie Baudoin Lebon, Paris, France (cat.)
"Sculpture/Nature," Centre d'Arts Plastiques Contemporains de Bordeaux, France (cat.)

"Architectural Analogues," Whitney Museum Downtown Branch, New York, NY (cat.)
"Made by Sculptors," Stedelijk Museum, Amsterdam, The Netherlands (cat.)
"Dwellings," Institute of Contemporary Art, University of Pennsylvania, Philadelphia, PA (circulated: Neuberger Museum, State University of New York, College at Purchase, NY) (cat.)
"Venice Biennale," Italy (cat.)
"Quintessence," Wright State University and the City Beautiful Council, Dayton, OH
Rosa Esman Gallery, New York, NY
"DAAD Artists," DAADgalerie, West Berlin, West Germany
"Dokumenta 6," Kassel, West Germany (cat.)
"Kunst und Architektur," Gallery Magers, Bonn, West Germany (cat.)
"Scale and Environment: 10 Sculptors," Walker Art Center, Minneapolis, MN (cat.)
1978- "Probing the Earth: Contemporary Land Projects," Hirshhorn
77   Museum and Sculpture Garden, Smithsonian Institution, Washington, D.C. (circulated: La Jolla Museum of Contemporary Art, CA; Seattle Art Museum, WA)
1977   "The Whitney Biennial Exhibition of Painting and Sculpture," Whitney Museum of American Art, New York, NY (cat.)
"A Question of Scale," Visual Arts Museum, New York, NY
1976   "Scale," Fine Arts Building, New York, NY
"Personal Mythologies," Fine Arts Building, New York, NY
"9e Biennale de Paris à Nice," Musées de Nice, France (cat.)
"Earth Day Festival, 1976," American Museum of Natural History, New York, NY
"Venice Biennale," Italy (cat.)
1975   "The Whitney Biennial Exhibition of Painting and Sculpture," Whitney Museum of American Art, New York, NY (cat.)
Artists' Space, New York, NY
112 Greene Street, New York, NY
"9e Biennale de Paris," Musée d'Art Moderne de la Ville de Paris, France (cat.)
"Art in Landscape" (circulated by Independent Curators, Inc., Washington, D.C.) (cat.)
"Not Photography," Fine Arts Building, New York, NY
"Small Scale," The Art Institute of Chicago, IL (cat.)
1974   "Interventions in Landscape," Hayden Gallery, Massachusetts Institute of Technology, Cambridge, MA (cat.)
1973   "8e Biennale de Paris," Musée d'Art Moderne de la Ville de Paris, France (cat.)

WORKS IN THE EXHIBITION

"On-Site Installation," 1982 (plate 49, cat. only)
Site: Los Angeles County Museum of Art, CA
Photograph courtesy of Los Angeles County Museum of Art, CA

"Dwelling, La Biennale di Venezia," 1978*
20″ × 30″ × 10″ (approx.), clay bricks, ½″ long each
Site: Venice, Italy

"Circles and Towers Growing, No. 6 (Untitled)," 1978*
6″ × 30″ × 30″ (approx.), clay, sand, pebbles, sticks, bones and shells on plywood

Video tape of two films:

"Dwellings Winter 1974," 1974
Color, 13 minutes
Filmed and edited by Rudolph Burckhardt

"Landscape–Body–Dwelling," 1973
Color, 7 minutes
Filmed by Rudolph Burckhardt, edited by Charles Simonds

Video tape reproduction: Museum of Contemporary Art, Chicago, IL

CHARLES SIMONDS

PLATE 50   *CORDOBA*, 1983
PLATE 51   *SICILIANA*, 1983

STATEMENT

My work is based on the idea of architectural fragments as sculpture. The sculpture is constructed with modules which are the actual size of bricks (8″×4″×2″). In addition, I am concerned with how the work relates to space. The scale and size of each piece, as well as the spatial relationships among elements, are determined by the given space. Due to the nature of the material used, ¼-inch wire mesh, the viewers will experience different visual phenomena, such as moving moire patterns, varying degrees of transparencies and transformation of the material itself (from metallic to glassy). As the viewers move through or pass by the work, they will see suspended planes instead of three-dimensional forms. Light plays an important role on my sculpture; it can render the work more illusionistic and less physical and tangible if strong light is directed towards it.

Kit-Yin Tieng Snyder, 1983

SELECTED BIOGRAPHY

Born in Canton, China
Lives in New York, New York

Selected Honors

1983 International Water Sculpture, winner, New Orleans World Exposition (1984), LA
1982 National Endowment for the Arts, Artist's Fellowship
1981 New York State Council on the Arts, Creative Artists Public Service Grant, Sculpture
Artist-in-Residence, Bryant Park, New York, NY (sponsored by the Public Art Fund for the construction of large temporary outdoor sculpture)
1980 National Endowment for the Arts, Artist's Fellowship
1979 P.S. 1 Studio Residency Grant, The Institute for Art and Urban Resources, Long Island City, NY
1974 National Endowment for the Arts, Craftsman's Fellowship

Selected Solo Site Works

1983 "Hong Kong, Tokyo, New York," Kenkeleba Gallery, ArtPark, Lewiston, NY
Federal Hall National Memorial, New York, NY
"Cordoba," City University Center, City University, New York, NY
1982 "Cloister," Just Above Midtown/Downtown Gallery, New York, NY
1979 "Installation of Sculpture," Lang Music Building, Swarthmore College, PA

Selected Site Work

1983 Art in Architecture Program, VA Hospital Nursing Home, Dallas, TX (completion 1984)

Selected Group Exhibitions

1983 "Shared Space," ("Overture"), Bronx Museum, NY
"Air and Ice," Lake George, NY
"4th Texas Sculpture Symposium," Huntington Gallery, University of Texas, Austin, TX
1982 "Ten Years of Public Art," Doris Freedman Gallery, The Urban Center, New York, NY
"Monument Redefined," Gowanus Memorial Artyard, Brooklyn, NY
1981 "Environmental Interplay—7 Sculptors," Alternative Museum, New York, NY
"Installation of Sculpture," New York State Council on the Arts, Creative Artists Public Service Grant, Sculpture, Arnot Museum, Elmira, NY
"Made in Philadelphia," Institute of Contemporary Art, University of Pennsylvania, Philadelphia, PA
1980 "Architectural Sculpture," Los Angeles Institute of Contemporary Art, CA (cat.)
"Drawing Done by Sculptors," United Arts Building, Philadelphia, PA
"P.S. 1—IV," Room 303, The Institute for Art and Urban Resources, Long Island City, NY
1979 "Second Biennial Exhibition," ARCO Center for Visual Art, Los Angeles, CA
"Black and White are Colors," Lang Art Gallery, Claremont, CA

Selected Public Collections

Lannan Foundation, Palm Beach, FL
Utah Museum of Fine Arts, University of Utah, Salt Lake City, UT
Wilmington Museum of Fine Arts, DE
Newark Museum, NJ

WORKS IN THE EXHIBITION

"Untitled," 1983
9'6″×10'6″×7' (approx.), galvanized steel wire mesh and wood base
Site: California State University, Fullerton, CA

"Cordoba," 1983 (plate 50, cat. only)
9'6″×65' (space), galvanized steel wire mesh
Site: City University Center, City University, New York, NY
Photographed by Kit-Yin Tieng Snyder

"Siciliana," 1983 (plate 51, cat. only)
9'6″×45'×60' (space), galvanized steel wire mesh and pine trees
Site: ArtPark, Lewiston, NY
Photographed by Kit-Yin Tieng Snyder

"Cloister," 1982*
9'×25'×25,' galvanized steel wire mesh
Site: Just Above Midtown/Downtown Gallery, New York, NY

KIT-YIN TIENG SNYDER

PLATE 52   *FLOWERING HOUSE*, 1983

STATEMENT

I just kept coming up with the fact that we are all houses, and so is everything else in the universe. What is not a house for something? What does not live in something? I just believe that every molecule houses something—and there are doorways to enter or leave it all.

James Surls, 1983

SELECTED BIOGRAPHY

Born in Terrell, Texas, 1943
Lives in Splendora, Texas

Selected Solo Exhibitions

1982 Allan Frumkin Gallery, New York, NY
      Akron Art Museum, OH
      St. Louis Art Museum, MO
1981 Delahunty Gallery, Dallas, TX
      Daniel Weinberg Gallery, San Francisco, CA
1980 Allan Frumkin Gallery, New York, NY
1979 Delahunty Gallery, Dallas, TX
      Robinson Galleries, Houston, TX
1977 Delahunty Gallery, Dallas, TX
      Contemporary Arts Museum, Houston, TX
1975 Contemporary Arts Museum, Houston, TX
      Austin College, Sherman, TX
1974 Tyler Museum of Art, TX
      Delahunty Gallery, Dallas, TX

Selected Group Exhibitions

1982 "20 American Artists: Sculpture 1982," San Francisco Museum of Modern Art, CA
      "Surls, Scanga, Lucero," Delahunty Gallery, Dallas, TX (circulated: Texas Gallery, Houston, TX)
1981 "A Sense of Spirit," University of Houston, Lawndale Annex, TX
      "Pegasus," Dallas City Hall, TX
      "The Image of the House in Contemporary Art," University of Houston, Lawndale Annex, TX (cat.)
1980 "Houston Exchange Show," 500 Exposition, Dallas, TX
      "Surls-Locke," University Center Art Gallery, Louisiana State University, Shreveport, LA
      "10 Abstract Sculptures," Max Hutchinson Gallery, New York, NY
1979 "The Whitney Biennial Exhibition of Painting and Sculpture," Whitney Museum of American Art, New York, NY
      "Fire," Contemporary Arts Museum, Houston, TX
1977 "Nine Artists: Theodoron Awards," The Solomon R. Guggenheim Museum, New York, NY
      "Artists' Biennial," New Orleans Museum of Art, LA
      "Installations in Corner Spaces," Fort Worth Art Museum, TX
1976 "Tex/Lax: Texas in L.A.," Union Gallery, California State University, Los Angeles, CA
      "Main Street 1976," Houston, TX
      "ArtPark 1976," The Program in the Visual Arts, Lewiston, NY
1975 "Exchange: DFW/SFO," Fort Worth Art Museum, TX (circulated)
      "Monumental Sculpture Exhibition," Houston, TX
1974 "First Biennial Invitational Painting and Sculpture Exhibition," Beaumont Art Museum, TX
      "Eighth Annual National Drawing and Small Sculpture Exhibition," Del Mar College, Corpus Christi, TX
      "Twelve–Texas," Contemporary Arts Museum, Houston, TX
1973 "Tarrant County Annual," Fort Worth Art Museum, TX
      "15th Annual Delta Art Exhibition," Little Rock, AR
      "839½ Exposition" (two-man show), Dallas, TX
      "Houston Designer Show," University of Houston, TX
1971 "12th Annual Painting and Sculpture Exhibition," Oklahoma Art Center, Oklahoma City, OK
      "15th Texas Crafts Exhibition," Dallas Museum of Fine Arts, TX
      "14th Annual Delta Art Exhibition," Little Rock, AR
1970 "11th Annual Painting and Sculpture Exhibition," Oklahoma Art Center, Oklahoma City, OK
1968 "14th Annual Drawing and Small Sculpture Show," Muncie, IN
      "3rd Biennial Michigan Artists," Grand Rapids, MI
      "Michianna Regional Art Exhibition," South Bend, IN
1967 "Bloomfield Art Association Sculpture Show," Bloomfield Hills, MI

WORKS IN THE EXHIBITION

"Flowering House," 1983 (plate 52)
15½" × 13" × 6½," wood
Photographed by Mark Schwartz

"Weathering the Storm," 1980*
120" × 132," cypress, pine and oak

JAMES SURLS

PLATE 53 *TALKING GARDEN*, 1982

100

STATEMENT

For over ten years my work has been characterized by two consistent elements: a longstanding interest in architecture and a fascination with the interface of Asian and Western cultures. I find the scale and functional aspects of architecture essential to creating the "worlds" my pieces suggest. Guided by my past experience in Asia, I make works that embrace a future in which I see East and West as ever closer. My works, whether temporary installations in galleries, individual architectural sculptures or outdoor public pieces, are site-specific. The walls and doors of an interior space or the nearby shrubs and trees of an outdoor location are as much a part of the piece as what I construct myself. I design my works so that they are both accessible enough to encourage participation and subtle enough for the audience to find room for its own response and interpretation within the "world" of the piece.

Richard Turner, 1983

SELECTED BIOGRAPHY

Born in Kansas City, Missouri, 1943
Lives in Orange, California

Selected Honors
1983   Louisiana World Exposition Water Sculpture Competition, finalist
1981   National Endowment for the Arts, Artist's Fellowship
1968   Horace H. Rackham Grant
1967   Fulbright Fellowship

Selected Solo Exhibitions
1983- "Reliquaries," Baxter Art Gallery, California Institute of Tech-
82   nology, Pasadena, CA
1981   "Bivouac," Works, San Jose, CA
       "Immolation Maze," Fine Arts Gallery, Mount St. Mary's College, Los Angeles, CA (cat.)
       "Richard Turner/Bruce Williams," Stage One Gallery, Orange, CA
1972   "Orange Grove Rip-off," Purcell Gallery, Chapman College, Orange, CA

Selected Group Exhibitions
1982   "Estuary Channel Sculpture Project," The Oakland Museum, CA
       "Forgotten Dimension . . . A Survey of Small Sculpture in California Now," Fresno Arts Center, CA (circulated: San Francisco International Airport, CA; Center for the Visual Arts, Illinois State University, Normal, IL) (cat.)
1980   "Architectural Sculpture," Fine Arts Gallery, University of California, Irvine, CA, and Chapman College, Orange, CA (two installations, organized by Los Angeles Institute of Contemporary Art, CA) (cat.)
1979   "Recent Coincidences," Union Gallery, California State University, San Jose, CA
       "Our Own Artists: Art in Orange County" (with Bruce Williams), Newport Harbor Art Museum, Newport Beach, CA (cat.)
1979- "Rooms: Moments Remembered," Newport Harbor Art Museum,
78   Newport Beach, CA (cat.)
1977   "XEROX, XEROX, XEROX," University of Boulder, CO (cat.)
       "Images: Interior/Exterior," Municipal Art Gallery, Barnsdall Park, Los Angeles, CA
       "Proposal 1-5," Union Gallery, California State University, San Jose, CA (cat.)
1976   "California Hawaii Biennial 1976," Fine Arts Gallery of San Diego, Balboa Park, CA (cat.)
       "The Printed Work," La Mamelle, Inc., San Francisco, CA
1975   "Photographics," Gallery 58F, Orange, CA
       "Object/Subject," Los Angeles Institute of Contemporary Art, CA (cat.)
1974   "Tongue in Groove," Art Gallery, Santa Ana College, CA
       "Group Drawing Exhibition," Gallery 58F, Orange, CA
1973   "East/West: Cultural Interface in the Arts of Southern California," Purcell Gallery, Chapman College, Orange, CA

Selected Film and Video
1980   "Spring Snow/Forbidden Colors" (film)
1978   "Episodes in Language and Perception" (video)
1976   "Double Suicide" (video)
1975   "Thermal Tests" (film)
       "Domestic Demonstrations" (film)
       "Fortune Cookies" (video)
1974   "Chinese Restaurants in Los Angeles and Orange County" (film)
       "1000 Arts Journal" (film)
1972   "The Ropetones" (film)
       "Indian Painting as Seen Through Episodes from the Ramayana" (film)
       "Geisha Girl" (film)
       "Orientation Film" (film)
1970   "Sword Drill" (film)
       "Kali Yuga" (film)
       "Check in Time" (video)
1969   "Everstar" (video)

Selected Performances
1979   "Vietnamese Art Lessons," Palos Verdes Art Center, CA
1977   "Spring Snow/Forbidden Colors," Guggenheim Gallery, Chapman College, Orange, CA
1974   "Greater Los Angeles Zen Promo," Immaculate Heart College, Los Angeles, CA
1973   "Third Eye Round Up," (circulated: University of California, Irvine, CA; California State University, Los Angeles, CA; Immaculate Heart College, Los Angeles, CA; Golden West College, Huntington Beach, CA)
1972   "The Cue Spot," Cue Spot Bar, Orange, CA

WORKS IN THE EXHIBITION

"Wall Gazing Gallery," 1983
12' x 12' x 14,' Douglas fir, corrugated iron, enamel, paint and water
Site: California State University, Fullerton, CA

"Talking Garden" (with Douglas Hollis), 1982 (plate 53)*
40' x 80,' pine, aluminum, fiberglass, steel and water
Site: The Oakland Museum, CA
Photographed by M. Lee Fatherree

RICHARD TURNER

PLATE 54   *THE DANCING TEACHER*, 1972

102

STATEMENT

Westermann's approach to making sculpture is intuitive, and what emerges from his art process is a highly charged yet completely enigmatic object. He does not materialize a preexisting concept; it is only as he works on a piece that its configuration and "idea" emerge. An initial impulse will suggest a piece, but actual construction often triggers a series of intuitive associations which lead to an object quite different from the original motivation. The work evolves through unconscious associations rather than through an analytic progression of thoughts, so that even Westermann himself cannot articulate exactly how he arrives at the finished object or precisely what it means.

From Barbara Haskell in *H.C. Westermann*, Whitney Museum of American Art (New York, 1978), p. 21.

SELECTED BIOGRAPHY

Born in Los Angeles, California, 1922
Died in 1981

Selected Honors

1968 Tamarind Fellowship
1967 National Endowment for the Arts, Artist's Fellowship
1964 Campana Memorial Prize
1960 New Talent Award, *Art in America*

Selected Solo Exhibitions

1979- "H.C. Westermann," Whitney Museum of American Art, New
78 York, NY (circulated: New Orleans Museum of Art, LA; Des Moines Art Center, IA; Seattle Art Museum, WA; San Francisco Museum of Modern Art, CA) (cat.)
1977 "The Connecticut Ballroom: A Portfolio of Six Woodcuts," John Berggruen Gallery, San Francisco, CA
1976 "H.C. Westermann: New Works," Allan Frumkin Gallery, Chicago, IL
1974 "H.C. Westermann," James Corcoran Gallery, Los Angeles, CA
"H.C. Westermann, New Sculptures and Drawings," Allan Frumkin Gallery, New York, NY
1973 "H.C. Westermann," Galerie Neuendorf, Hamburg, West Germany
1973, "H.C. Westermann," Allan Frumkin Gallery, Chicago, IL
71
1973, "H.C. Westermann," Allan Frumkin Gallery, New York, NY
71,70
1972 "H.C. Westermann," Galerie Rudolf Zwirner, Cologne, West Germany
1970 "H.C. Westermann Drawings," Galerie Thomas Borgmann, Cologne, West Germany
1968 "H.C. Westermann," Los Angeles County Museum of Art, CA (circulated: Museum of Contemporary Art, Chicago, IL) (cat.)
1966 "H.C. Westermann," Kansas City Art Institute, MO

Selected Group Exhibitions

1981 "The Image of the House in Contemporary Art," University of Houston, Lawndale Annex, Houston, TX (cat.)
1977 "A View of a Decade," Museum of Contemporary Art, Chicago, IL (cat.)
"The Whitney Biennial Exhibition of Painting and Sculpture," Whitney Museum of American Art, New York, NY
1976 "Venice Biennale," Italy (cat.)
"200 Years of American Sculpture," Whitney Museum of American Art, New York, NY (cat.)
1975 "Masterworks in Wood: The Twentieth Century," Portland Art Museum, OR (cat.)
"Sculpture: American Directions, 1945–1975," National Collection of Fine Arts, Smithsonian Institution, Washington, D.C.
1974 "Made in Chicago: Some Resources," National Collection of Fine Arts, Smithsonian Institution, Washington, D.C. (circulated: Museum of Contemporary Art, Chicago, IL) (cat.)
1973 "Extraordinary Realities," Whitney Museum of American Art, New York, NY (circulated: Everson Museum of Art of Syracuse and Onondaga County, NY)

"XII Bienal de São Paulo," Brazil (circulated: Museo de Arte Moderno, Bogota, Columbia; Museo Nacional de Bellas Artes, Santiago, Chile; Museo Nacional de Bellas Artes, Buenos Aires, Argentina; Museu de Arte Moderno, Mexico City, Mexico)
"The Whitney Biennial Exhibition of Painting and Sculpture," Whitney Museum of American Art, New York, NY
1972 "Chicago Imagist Art," Museum of Contemporary Art, Chicago, IL (cat.)
"10 Independents: An Artist-Initiated Exhibition," The Solomon R. Guggenheim Museum, New York, NY (cat.)

WORKS IN THE EXHIBITION

"Dovetail House," 1979*
14" × 19" × 20," pine, glass, enamel and lead

"Snake House," 1976*
12" × 14" × 8," bird's-eye maple

"The Dancing Teacher," 1972 (plate 54)**
21" × 28" × 17¾," copper screen, glass, lead and wood
Lent by Edwin Janss
Photographed by Tom Vinetz

"Mad House," 1958*
39½" × 20" × 20," Douglas fir, glass, metal and enamel

"Mysterious Yellow Mausoleum," 1958*
49" high; Douglas fir, metal, tar and enamel

"Old Eccentric's House," 1956–57*
18½" × 18⅞" × 33¼," spruce lath and mirror

H.C. WESTERMANN

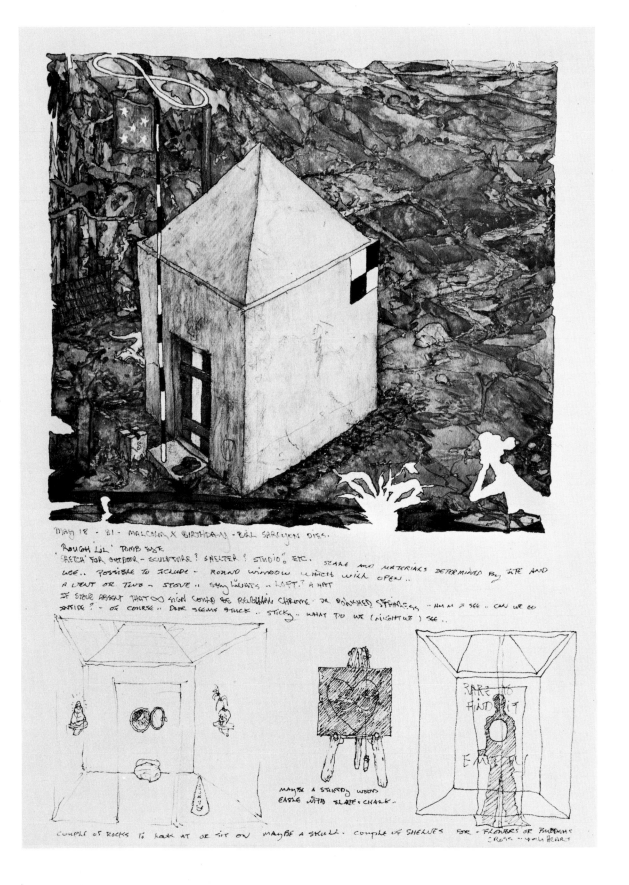

PLATE 55   *TOMB EYE SKETCH,* 1981

104

STATEMENT

I.T.H.A.G. The House That Art Built . .
to take care of itself? Dry spot on occassion
out of the (rain . . wind . . whatever . . . .)
Don't want to be tied or tardy with em . .
struck sure on the shimmering plain.
Grateful at times . . tired "sleep„, andreams!!
. . Thankfull for the mother ship . .
an imagined skin so real o agaiñ
housing feelings. And all imagined forms of
protection . . up to snuff.

      Skincerely

Who the house?
Who the housed?
S P E A K !

P.S. Maybe it's just for the muse-
seeum

William T. Wiley, 1983

SELECTED BIOGRAPHY
Born in Bedford, Indiana, 1937
Lives in Forest Knolls, California

Selected Honors
1980 Australian Arts Council, travel grant
1976 William H. Bartels Prize, "Seventy-second American Exhibition,"
The Art Institute of Chicago, IL
1968 Purchase Prize, Whitney Museum of American Art, New
York, NY
Nealie Sullivan Award, San Francisco Art Institute, CA
1962 Sculpture Prize, Los Angeles County Museum of Art, CA
1961 New Talent Award, *Art in America*

Selected Solo Exhibitions
1981 "William T. Wiley," Florida State University, Tallahassee, FL
(circulated: Florida International University, Miami, FL;
University of Southern Florida, Tampa, FL) (cat.)
1981, Allan Frumkin Gallery, New York, NY
79
1981- "William T. Wiley, Graphics 1967–1979," Landfall Press,
80 Chicago, IL (circulated) (cat.)
"William Wiley: Twelve Years"(circulated: Dallas Museum of
Fine Arts, TX; The Denver Art Museum, CO; Des Moines Art
Center, IA; San Francisco Museum of Modern Art, CA; Phoenix
Art Museum, AZ) (cat.)
1980 "William T. Wiley," The Charles H. Scott Gallery, Emily Carr
College of Art, Vancouver, British Columbia, Canada (circulated:
Allan Frumkin Gallery, New York, NY) (cat.)
"William T. Wiley," John Buckley for Realities Gallery, Mel-
bourne, Australia (circulated: Institute of Modern Art, Brisbane,
Queensland, Australia)
1980, Hansen Fuller Gallery, San Francisco, CA
78
1979 "William T. Wiley: Prints," Landfall Press, Chicago, IL (circulated: Baltimore Museum of Art, MD)
1979, Allan Frumkin Gallery, Chicago, IL
74
1976 The Museum of Modern Art, Project Room, New York, NY
Allan Frumkin Gallery, New York, NY
1977 "William T. Wiley," Galerie Paul Facchetti, Paris, France (cat.)
"Suite of Daze," The Art Institute of Chicago, IL
1976 Margo Leavin Gallery, Los Angeles, CA
75,72
1975, Hansen Fuller Gallery, San Francisco, CA
74
1973 "William T. Wiley," Stedelijk van Abbemuseum, Eindhoven, The
Netherlands (cat.)
1972 "William T. Wiley," Gallerie Odyssia, Rome, Italy (cat.)
1972- "William T. Wiley," University Art Museum, University of
California, Berkeley, CA (circulated: The Art Institute of Chicago,
IL; Corcoran Gallery of Art, Washington, D.C.) (cat.)

Selected Group Exhibitions
1982 "Western American Art in California Collections," Palm Springs
Desert Museum, CA (cat.)
1981 "Drawing Acquisitions 1978–1981," Whitney Museum of American Art, New York, NY (cat.)
1981- "Drawings: The Pluralist Decade," 39th Venice Biennale, United
80 States Pavilion, Italy (circulated: Institute of Contemporary Art,
University of Pennsylvania, Philadelphia, PA; Museum of Contemporary Art, Chicago, IL) (cat.)
1981- "The 1970s: New American Painting," organized by The New
79 Museum, New York, NY (circulated: Eastern Europe)
"The First Western States Biennial Exhibition," Western States
Art Foundation, Denver, CO (circulated: Seattle Art Museum,
WA; San Francisco Museum of Modern Art, CA; National Collec-
tion of Fine Arts, Smithsonian Institution, Washington,
D.C.) (cat.)
1981 "The Image of the House in Contemporary Art," University of
Houston, Lawndale Annex, TX (cat.)
1980 "AZ 1970—Es Evek Uj Amerikai Festeszete," Hungary (organized
by The New Museum, New York, NY)
"Prints from the Landfall Press: A Gift from Allan Frumkin," The
David and Alfred Smart Gallery, University of Chicago, IL
"American Painting of the '60s and '70s: The Real, The Ideal, The
Fantastic" (selections from the Whitney Museum of American
Art), Montgomery Museum of Fine Arts, AL (cat.)
1979- "American Painting of the 1970s," Albright-Knox Art Gallery,
78 Buffalo, NY (circulated: Newport Harbor Art Museum, Newport
Beach, CA; Cincinnati Art Museum, OH; Art Museum of South-
ern Texas, Corpus Christi, TX; Krannert Art Museum, Univer-
sity of Illinois, Champaign, IL) (cat.)
1979- "American Drawing 1927–77," Minnesota Museum of Art,
77 St. Paul, MN (circulated: Europe)
"American Narrative/Story Art: 1967–1977," Contemporary Art
Museum, Houston, TX (circulated: Winnipeg Art Gallery, Winni-
peg, Manitoba, Canada; University Art Museum, University of
California, Berkeley, CA; Art Gallery, University of California,
Santa Barbara, CA (cat.)
1978 "6th International Exhibition of Original Drawings," Museum of
Modern Art, Rijeka, Yugoslavia (cat.)
"Aesthetics of Graffiti," San Francisco Museum of Modern Art,
CA (cat.)
"California: 3 × 8 Twice," Honolulu Academy of Arts, HI (cat.)
1977 "Recent Art from San Francisco," Den Haag, Amsterdam, The
Netherlands
"Drawings of the '70s," Society of Contemporary Art, The Art
Institute of Chicago, IL

WORK IN THE EXHIBITION

"Tomb Eye Sketch," 1981 (plate 55)*
30" × 22," watercolor and ink on paper
Photographed by M. Lee Fatherree

05

WILLIAM T. WILEY

ACKNOWLEDGMENTS

Art Gallery Director
Dextra Frankel
Assistant to the Director
Marilyn Moore
Exhibition Organization and Selection
Dextra Frankel

Catalogue and Announcement Design
Jerry Samuelson
Announcement Illustration Production
Larry Johnson
Catalogue and Announcement Printing
Haddad's Fine Arts, Inc., Anaheim
Catalogue Editing
Barbara McAlpine, La Habra
Compilation and Research
Kerry Boyd
Tina Yapelli
Compilation Assistants
Marilyn Moore
Debra Williams
Eric Gaard
Anthony C.H. Fung
Joseph Silvestri
Bridget Ritter
Susan Melton
Essays
Foreword, "The Architecture Within," Dextra Frankel,
Laguna Beach, 1983
"On Place and Space," Jan Butterfield,
San Francisco, 1983
"The House That Art Built," Michael H. Smith,
Pasadena, 1983
Typesetting
Barbara McAlpine Typography, La Habra
Typefaces: Helios Condensed II and Garth Graphic
Production
Kerry Boyd
Anthony C.H. Fung

Slide-Sound Presentation Coordinator
Tina Yapelli
Script and Production
Tina Yapelli
Kerry Boyd
Eric Gaard
Production Assistants
Marianne Lamb
Bridget Ritter
Sound Production and Technical Assistance
John R. Fisher, CSUF Theatre Arts Department
Narration
James Matthis
Roland Reiss
Roland Reiss Interview
Tina Yapelli
Eric Gaard

Historical Reference
Giotto
Paul Cézanne
René Magritte
Charles Sheeler
Edward Hopper
Andrew Wyeth
Anonymous children
Music
From *Trans-Europe-Express*, Kraftwerk
From *Glassworks*, Philip Glass

Exhibition Design
Dextra Frankel
Art Gallery Staff Technician
D. Gene Karraker
Art Gallery Staff
Kerry Boyd
Craig Hollingsworth
Lynn LaBate
David Messenger
Bruce Stowell
Debra Williams
Tina Yapelli
Installation Assistants
Lance Benson
Anthony C.H. Fung
Norma Hawkins
Eileen Hook
Susan Melton
Bridget Ritter
Joseph Silvestri

Symposium
Friday, November 11, 1983
9:30 a.m.–12:30 p.m.
University Center, Multipurpose Rooms A/B
Moderator
Jan Butterfield, Associate Editor, *Images & Issues*
Panelists
Siah Armajani
Tony Berlant
Roland Reiss
Elyse Grinstein
Paul Schimmel

Site and Installation Works Executed for "The House That Art Built"
Edward Mayer, sculpture court
Kit-Yin Tieng Snyder, Art Gallery entrance
Richard Turner, Visual Arts Center, plaza reflective pool

Sponsors
National Endowment for the Arts, Washington, D.C. a
federal agency
Instructionally Related Activities Committee
Associated Students
Art Alliance
Department of Art
School of the Arts